TEACHING OF WORLD HISTORY

Gerald Leinwand

Bulletin 54

NATIONAL COUNCIL FOR THE SOCIAL STUDIES

ABOUT THE AUTHOR

Gerald Leinwand is President of Oregon College of Education in Monmouth. He is author of *The Pageant of World History*; *The Pageant of American History* (Allyn and Bacon); co-author of *Teaching History and the Social Studies* (Pitman); and author-editor of the *Problems of American Society* series (Simon and Schuster).

Library of Congress Catalog Card Number: 77-95099
ISBN 0-87986-019-7
Copyright © 1978 by the
NATIONAL COUNCIL FOR THE SOCIAL STUDIES
2030 M Street, N.W. Washington, D.C. 20036

Foreword

Fourteen years have passed since the National Council for the Social Studies has released a major publication on the teaching of World History. Yet the importance of helping students to understand other cultures and the dynamics of global affairs has been underscored by events of the intervening years. Long held assumptions about the relative prestige and power of nations have been undermined by shifts in economic and political conditions. The language of diplomacy and trade—once French, later English—may soon be Arabic. Advances in space technology have opened up for us new perspectives on the universe at a time when we are still groping for an understanding of the dramatic changes taking place on our own planet.

The study of World History has an important place. As Shirley Engle wrote in 1965, "The particular contribution of world history lies in the broad view of humanity . . . which it affords." Certainly, an understanding of the ways human beings have responded to their environments and of the social, political, and economic arrangements they have created is fundamental to intelligent participation in the global community.

In this bulletin Gerald Leinwand brings together practical materials and approaches for the teaching of World History. Secondary school teachers in particular will find the variety of specific examples, guidelines, and suggestions useful. For all those who are concerned with revising or reviving the teaching of World History, this bulletin should serve as a helpful resource. The National Council for the Social Studies is grateful to Gerald Leinwand for this contribution to the improvement of World History instruction.

Anna S. Ochoa, *President*
National Council for the Social Studies

Preface

Among the objectives of a high school curriculum are to provide students with a world-wide perspective, and to develop catholic interests and global horizons. While in a certain sense each subject of the secondary school curriculum is expected to make some contribution toward these objectives, probably no single subject bears a greater responsibility than does the world history course of study. Yet, few subjects have been more severely criticized by teachers, as well as by laymen; and few subjects have been more thoroughly disliked by students.

This bulletin on the teaching of world history assumes that such a course is both teachable and worth teaching. It postulates three basic principles:

1. Before students and teachers can understand and appreciate they must know.

2. The question is central to the teaching of world history, both the question the teacher poses and the question the student raises.

3. As important as it is to decide what to teach, it is equally important to decide what to leave out.

These principles are not new, but they have often been ignored in the search for alternative teaching methods. Innovative approaches to the teaching of world history are much to be desired, but there is no alternative to scholarly competence both on the part of the teacher and on the part of those taught.

This bulletin owes a great deal to the many social studies teachers with whom I have worked over the years, and to the many college students preparing to teach social studies for whose training and education I have had some responsibility at both The City College of New York and The Bernard M. Baruch College, both of The City University of New York. Specifically, I wish to thank William S. Dobkin, Chairman of the Social Studies Department of Francis Lewis High School; Leon Hellerman, Chairman of the Social Studies Department of George W. Hewlett High School; Daniel Feins, Principal of Walton High School, with whom I wrote *Teaching History and the Social Studies*, from which portions of this bulletin have been drawn; and Patricia O'Connor for the skillful editing and typing of the manuscript. I am grateful also to Daniel Roselle, editor of *Social Education*, and to the National Council for the Social Studies for the opportunity of reviewing the world history course of study and the ways of teaching it. It was an enriching and rewarding experience and very much welcomed.

Gerald Leinwand
New York

Contents

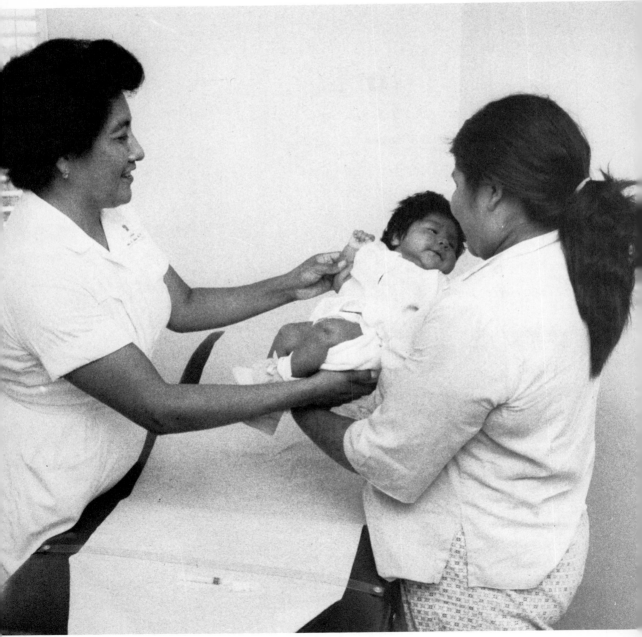

1

World History: Today and Tomorrow

The class, consisting of seventeen boys and fifteen girls, is discussing how a "document," reproduced and distributed to them by their teacher, Ms. Silver, may be identified and how its significance as an historical source may be ascertained. The document, from which all identifying and chronological references had been removed, reads as follows:

When he was brought to Westminister Hall, before the high court of justice, he looked upon them and sat down without any manifestation of trouble, never doffing his hat. He was impeached for treasons and crimes as a tyrant, traitor and murderer, and a public enemy to the commonwealth. President Bradshaw, after he had insolently reprimanded him for not having doffed his hat or showing more respect, asked what answer he made to that impeachment.

He told them he would first know of them by what authority they presumed by force to bring him before them, and who gave them power to judge his actions, for which he was accountable to none but God. He told them that they owed him duty and obedience; that no parliament had authority to call him before them. As there were many persons present at that woeful spectacle who felt a real compassion for him, so there were others of so barbarous and brutal a behavior toward him that they called him murderer; and one spat in his face which he without expressing any resentment wiped off with his handkerchief.

Of the execution and sentence no more shall be said here of that lamentable tragedy, so much to the dishonor of the nation.[1]

Ms. Silver: Can any of you identify the event to which the description refers? (*The class begins to read silently, and Ms. Silver, slowly and unobtrusively, walks about the room making mental notes of the reading habits of her class, observing the expressions on their faces, glowering when necessary so that talkative students "cease and desist" and apply themselves to the task at hand, and in general making her presence felt so that the atmosphere is purposeful. Slowly, several hands go up as some students feel they have an answer. Ms. Silver begins calling upon them.*) Alvin?

Alvin: It seems to me that this is a trial in France or some place. It seems to be a court scene, isn't it?

Ms. Silver: Well, let's see how the rest of you feel. Do you agree with Alvin, Tom?

Tom (*Tom has not raised his hand and is a bit startled at having been called upon*): Yeah, I do kinda! It's a description of a king's trial?

---

[1]Adapted from Edward Hyde, "The History of the Rebellion," in Hutton Webster, ed., *Readings in Medieval and Modern History*. Boston: D.C. Heath and Company, 1917.

1

Ms. Silver: How do you know?

Tom: It says so. Doesn't it?

Ms. Silver: Where?

Tom *(Scans the passage)*: It doesn't say so, but it seems that way.

Ms. Silver: Arlene?

Arlene: I agree with Tom. It doesn't say, but something tells me that it's a king all right. But not in France.

Margaret: I think it's a king's trial too, but we'd have to know more before we can be sure.

Ms. Silver: What do we need to know?

Margaret: Certainly we need to know where it happened. And when, too.

Jill: We need to know who is on trial, and knowing when and where the trial took place would help us.

Ms. Silver *(She had written the three questions on the board)*: Are there any additional questions you would want to ask? Jennie?

Jennie: Wouldn't we want to know why he was tried?

Jerome: And we would want to know who's trying him—what court or judge or something.

Andy: Who wrote this description? Did you write it, Ms. Silver?

Ms. Silver *(Joins the class in a guffaw of laughter)*: No, I didn't write it, but surely we'd want to know who did. You people are becoming real detectives. Ingemar?

Ingemar: Who's Bradshaw? That might be important.

Ms. Silver: That's a good point, Ingemar, as are the others. There are at least three basic questions: "What is the document?" "What episode does it describe?" "What is its value for history?" How would an historian go about trying to discover the answers to at least some of these questions?

The remainder of the session is devoted to a discussion of these and related questions, and the assignment given to the class is to try to identify the document using the clues provided by it.

The Past Is Prologue

"History," wrote Jacob Burckhardt, "is the record of what one age finds worthy of note in another."[2] Such a definition implies a flexible approach to the study and teaching of world history, since what one age finds worthy of note in another will vary from one generation to the next. In the classroom dialogue above, the teacher and class found the firsthand account of the behavior of Charles I at the time of his beheading worth noting and studying. Some other teacher and some other class might find other documents useful for their purposes. Thus, an intimate relationship exists between the past and the present, and in a sense history may be said to be as much a study of the present as it is of the past. What one generation finds worthy of note in another is at least as revealing of present attitudes, values, ideals, ambitions, and aspirations as it is of the past, which it also tries to understand.

Edward Hallett Carr in *What Is History?* saw the intimate relation between the past and the present, between history and modern society. "History is a continuous process of interaction between the present and the past."[3] "We can view the past and achieve our understanding of the past," wrote Carr, "only through the eyes of the present. . . .The very words. . .democracy, empire, war, revolution, have a current connotation from which we cannot divorce them."[4] And, St. Augustine, hundreds of years ago, echoed this view elegantly but succinctly when he wrote, "Time is a threefold present. The present as we experience it, the past as present memory, the future as present expectation."

Lest the teaching of world history become the mere recounting of "one damned thing after another," it is essential that the teacher of world history understand the relationship between the past and the present and adopt, adapt, or develop a conceptual framework about the nature of history and the nature of modern society. These mental images may then be used as yardsticks by which to measure the worth of what it is they choose to teach.

This chapter attempts a personal assessment of today's world. We start with the present because it is our present circumstance that will help determine what it is from the past that we will cull and teach. It is not important that the reader agree with all or with any of the judgments made here. But what is important is that some concept that may be the product of the teacher's own experience and reading must be developed in order to make wise judgments as to what in world history you will choose to teach and what you will decide to ignore.

In her well known and widely read book entitled *Rich Nations and Poor Nations*, Barbara Ward has identified four revolutions, already in progress, which are altering the ecological balance of our institutions and are reshaping the relationships among nations. A brief insight into these revolutions may help provide a meaningful backdrop against which to determine those portions of the world's history worth teaching. These revolutions Barbara Ward described as: (1) the idea of equality of men and nations; (2) the idea of progress; (3) the bio-

[2]H. R. Trevor-Roper in Jacob Burckhardt, *On History and Historians*. New York: Harper and Row, Harper Torchbooks, 1958, p. xi.

[3]Edward Hallett Carr, *What Is History?* New York: Alfred Knopf, 1963, p. 35.

[4]*Ibid.*, p. 28.

logical revolution; and (4) the application of science to nearly all forms of human effort and reason.

The Idea of
Equality of Men and Nations

The idea of equality is based on the principle in the Declaration of Independence which holds that "all men are created equal." What did the writers mean by equality, inasmuch as equality when they wrote the Declaration did not then exist in either what was to become the United States or in any other country of the world? In 1857 Abraham Lincoln offered an explanation of what the writers may have meant:

"I think," Lincoln said, "the authors of that notable instrument intended to include all men, but they did not intend to declare all men equal in all respects. They did not mean to say all were equal in color, size, intellect, moral development, or social capacity. They defined with tolerable distinctness in what respects they did consider all men created equal— equal in certain unalienable rights, among which are life, liberty and the pursuit of happiness. This they said, and this they meant."

Thus, according to Lincoln, that men were created equal meant only that they were equal before the law in their unalienable right to life and liberty and to pursue happiness as best they could.

Later on, the statement came to mean not merely equality before the law, but equality in the idea that all men and women should have equal opportunity for education and career. Today, this is probably still the dominant interpretation of the meaning of equality as that term is used in the Declaration of Independence. Although the idea of equality of opportunity has by no means been fully achieved, today there is a new concept. Not that all men are created equal, or are equal before the law, or should have equal opportunity, but that all people and all nations are equal. All men and women are equal, according to this view, without regard to sex, class, country of origin, race, wealth, intellectual or physical prowess or emotional stability. Politically, the concept is summarized as "one person, one vote"; and, on the international scene, manifests itself in the one nation, one vote provision found in the General Assembly of the United Nations.

However, "history points unmistakably to the fact that political democracy, in the forms in which it has hitherto been known, flourishes best where some of the people, but not all the people, are free and equal."[5] If this is so, how then shall we reconcile this lesson of history with the emergence of a mass civilization and popular sovereignty in which all people are equal and require and expect a full and equal role in determining their fate and in governing themselves?

Compounding the dilemma is the question of whether rational people can govern themselves and make wise judgments based on sound common sense on such highly complex questions as the arms race, détente and disarmament, the world-wide military industrial complex, international monetary agreements, the wise use of the world's resources, food for the hungry, and a better living standard for all. "If, as the old theories declared," worried Hallock Hoffman, "man is a rational political animal, he must then seek freedom and justice through his own thinking, talking and self-discipline. He had to govern himself, if he was to be himself. . .what if man's nature did require self-government, but man's situation no longer permitted it?"[6]

The Idea of Progress

From the earliest days of ancient Egypt, Greece, Rome, China, India, and through Europe's Middle Ages, there was little concern to improve conditions for the masses of humankind. For most centuries and for nearly all people, from the dawn of civilization to the Renaissance, people assumed that whatever was, was both inevitable and unavoidable. Men and women lived and died in the village where they were born, doing their work as their parents and grandparents had done before them, neither seeking nor expecting amelioration of their conditions.

Today, not only are people driven to be the equal of other people, but they are driv-

[5]Edward Hallett Carr, *The New Society*. Boston: Beacon Press, 1951, p. 61.
[6]In Scott Buchanan *et al.*, *Tragedy and the New Politics*. Santa Barbara, California: The Fund for the Republic, 1960, p. 2.

en also to make as much progress as other people. People translate that progress into material terms of consumer and capital goods—refrigerators and clothes washers, schools and factories. Nations translate the idea of progress into national armies and modern air forces they can usually ill afford. Thus, individuals of all countries, but perhaps most keenly in developing third and fourth world countries, measure their progress by the labor-saving devices which their political and economic systems provide. Governments measure progress by the industries, factories, and weaponry they can make—including the nuclear weapons they can develop. The people of every nation expect that they will inevitably have what the richest have, for this has been humankind's expectation at least since the sixteenth century. Today, there are probably no people on earth who are content with the *status quo*. None are content to do without the material benefits of civilization. Most people are obsessed with the idea that material progress can come quickly.

But are these yearnings for material goods likely to be fulfilled? This clamor for material well-being clashes head-on with what may be said to be the greatest ideological conflict of our time. Is our world one of finite or infinite resources? Are we about to be overtaken by the shades of Malthus, or are we on the threshold of a spectacular economic and technological advance in which all will share? There are some who hold that in a world of finite resources the people of the rich countries can only get richer at the expense of the poor, and that the poor can get richer only if the affluent agree to do with less. There are others who hold that the world's resources remain limitless and that science and technology will, as they have in the past, unlock new uses for, say, coal, the sun, or the atom; and that through the use of such resources, while the rich will get richer, the poor will also get richer.

That bigger and faster are always better, that tomorrow will always be better than today, that children will always live better than their parents are powerful ideas which the people of the western world have held for about 500 years. Today, in a world of seemingly finite resources, those ideas are brought into question. We question whether it is better to travel faster by SST (supersonic jet), if in doing so we destroy the environment. We doubt the desirability of ever larger governmental structures and giant industrial conglomerates. If resources continue to dwindle, our children may not enjoy the same high living standards we have enjoyed. Thus, there are clashing ideological cross-currents swirling about us; and little consensus appears to be developing as to what ought to be done or where these cross-currents are taking us. On the one hand, the developing nations, not having as yet achieved the living standards of the western world and Japan, are striving to catch up. Yet, what if catching up, in view of declining resources, is unlikely? In the developed countries, on the other hand, there is anxiety that further progress in traditional directions (bigger, more, faster, etc.) may no longer be possible. It is little wonder then that ours may be called *The Age of Uncertainty*, to use the title of one of John Kenneth Galbraith's works. To this age, the words of William Butler Yeats may be called to mind:

Things fall apart; the center cannot hold;
Mere anarchy is loosed upon the world;
The blood-dimmed tide is loosed, and everywhere
The ceremony of innocence is drowned;
The best lack all conviction, while the worst
Are full of passionate intensity.

The Biological Revolution

From the dawn of history the world's population grew slowly and steadily, so that in 1630 there were half a billion people. By 1830, however, there were one billion in the world; it had taken 200 years for the world's population to double. A hundred years later, in 1930, there were two billion people in the world; and in only 100 years the population doubled once again. Today, less than 50 years later, the world's population is over four billion. "At present rates of growth only fifteen more years will be needed to add the fifth billion. By the year 2000 it is estimated that there will be seven billion people on this planet."[7] These now familiar figures have vast implications.

[7]Harold F. Dorn, "World Population Growth," in Philip M. Hauser, ed., *The Population Dilemma*. New York: Prentice-Hall, 1963.

Since population growth is as much an incidence of a longer life span as anything else, it is apparent that there will be increasing numbers of people reaching middle and advanced years. Before long, we shall have a world population not only of unprecedented size, but one which may be polarized between youth and age. While the distribution between youth and age will vary from country to country in advanced countries with falling or steady birth rates, as in the United States and Sweden, there will be significant increases in the number of middle-aged and older people. How to reconcile the attitudes toward social needs between youth and age is something to which society must give increased attention.

Increased population will hasten the growth of cities. Urbanization, a world-wide phenomenon, is as much a characteristic of relatively less developed areas as it is of the great industrial nations. It is expected that the less developed nations of the world will experience an even more rapid rate of urbanization than the advanced countries where urbanization is already very far along. While rural life of less developed nations will by no means disappear, urbanization will provide an alternative life style for those who wish to choose it. "From Lagos to Singapore, from Manila to Zanzibar. . .the empty-bellied migrant from the land moves to the city in search of employment for himself, but for his children he is in search of education, the fulfillment of his twentieth-century city dreams in which each of his sons will be an urban professional, a lawyer, a doctor, an engineer, a politician, or a university professor."[8] By the year 2000, if present urbanization trends continue, New York and Tokyo will have been joined by at least 25 other contenders for the super-city class. Of these, no fewer than 18 will be in less developed countries. Mexico City, São Paulo, Shanghai, Peking, Bombay, Calcutta, Seoul, Buenos Aires, Rio de Janeiro, Cairo, Karachi, Teheran, New Delhi, Bangkok, Manilla, Lima, Bogota, and Jakarta are among those where the fastest growth is anticipated.

The implications for such developments are far-reaching. How to enable greatly enlarged populations to live in highly interactive environments without losing a sense of identity and privacy is not the least of these. How to govern vast urban complexes of which most nations are composed is an equally difficult problem. How to prevent government from becoming increasingly remote from people and how to enable citizens to participate more effectively in their governments may be regarded as an emerging dilemma for the people of the world.

The Application of Science and Technology

John Seeley, writing in *Daedalus* in 1968, had this to say; "What we have perfected is technology, and it is technology on which most men, most places, most times, rest such vague hopes as still stir. It is now almost in our hands to feed lavishly, clothe and render literate the world, to live in virtually instantaneous, universal, continuous, ubiquitous communication, to annihilate nearly all physical distance, to command more energy than we can use, to engineer mood and perhaps perception at will, to write genetic prescriptions as we wish, to make such men as whim may dictate. The universe capitulates. We are everywhere triumphant. But a premonitory smell of cosmic Neroism is in the air, and the cry of 'Stop the world; I want to get off' has become, whether absurd or not, pervasive and insistent."[9]

Theodore J. Gordon, in a selection entitled "The Feedback between Technology and Values," identified a number of developments which humankind may expect by the mid-21st century. He enumerated the more important of these as follows: fertility control, 100-year life span, personality control drugs, incapacitating rather than lethal weapons, ocean farming, controlled thermonuclear reactions, artificial life, weather control, genetic control, man-machine symbiosis, household robots, continued space exploration, ova/sperm banks. Which of these developments will actually materialize depends largely upon the values which

---

[8]David Lewis, "New Urban Structure," in Kurt Baier and Nicholas Rescher, eds., *Values and the Future*. New York: The Free Press, 1969, pp. 299–300.

[9]John R. Seeley, "Remaking the Urban Scene," *Daedalus*. Fall, 1968, p. 1133.

guide the decision-making process. While these technological developments will alter the values by which we live, the values by which we live will determine the kind of technological future that lies before us. Bertrand de Jouvenal has written: "No generation has been more free to lay the foundations of the good life, but we shall not be free if we do not become aware of our freedom."[10]

It is clear that the problems that trouble world society grow out of the fact that our value system, developed by a traditional world culture, has not yet adjusted to what Kenneth Boulding has called the superculture.

> The tensions between the superculture and traditional cultures are felt at a great many points. We see it, for instance, in the international system, where the superculture has given the traditional cultures of the nation appalling powers of destruction which are threatening the whole future of man. We see it in race relations, where the superculture moves towards uniformity, the absence of discrimination and differentiation by role rather than by race or class or other ascribed category. We see it in education, where formal education tends increasingly to become the agent of transmission of the superculture leaving the transmission of folk culture to the family, the peer group and more informal organizations. We see it in religion where the superculture tends towards the secular and the traditional culture preserves the sacred. . . . If the superculture simply destroys the traditional culture in which it is embedded, it may easily destroy itself. On the other hand, if the traditional culture does not adapt to the superculture, it too may destroy itself. This is a precarious balance, and not all societies may achieve it. The costs of a failure to achieve it are very high.[11]

The Telescoping of Revolutions

The revolutions thus far described are taking place concurrently and with lightning rapidity. What took centuries to achieve before takes only decades today. Charles Frankel, writing of "The Third Great Revolution of Mankind," describes this phenomenon as "the telescoping of revolutions." According to this view, the revolutionary cycle

completes itself in ever shorter intervals of time.

From about 500,000 B.C., humankind was essentially nomadic. By 25,000 B.C., what has been called "the Agricultural Revolution" began. That is, instead of wandering around from place to place for food to eat, men and women learned to farm the land, to cultivate the soil, and to grow food for themselves. This made settled communities possible. By 1750 A.D. or thereabouts, the so-called "Industrial Revolution" took place. This brought with it the application of machines of ever increasing sophistication to the labor of humankind. It lasted for but 150 years, when what might be called "the Space Revolution" began. Persons born at the turn of the century are still alive today to see the revolution implicit in humankind's conquest of space.

With each revolution in effect completing its cycle within the human life span, what is clear is that "the most vivid truth of our age is that no one will live all his life in the world in which he was born, and no one will die in the world in which he worked in his maturity."[12]

In view of this interpretation of our times, how will those of us who have trouble enough coping with our own world teach the history of humankind for an emerging world we cannot yet clearly see?

The Chinese said it was a curse to live in interesting times. Teaching world history in times of crises may be, if not a curse, at least an interesting challenge. In Chinese calligraphy, however, there is no one symbol for crisis. Instead, the ideograph is made up of two symbols, one of which when standing alone means danger; the other by itself means opportunity. Teaching world history today may thus be said to be both a danger as well as an opportunity, and therein lies the joy. Teachers of world history can take comfort from the lines of William Blake; for they, more than others, "hold infinity in the palm of [their] hand and eternity in an hour." Perhaps, then, the opportunities are greater than the dangers, and the class struggle well worth the effort.

[10]Bertrand de Jouvenal, "Technology as Means," in Kurt Baier and Nicholas Rescher, eds., *Values and the Future*. New York: The Free Press, 1969, p. 232.

[11]Kenneth Boulding, "The Emerging Superculture," in *op. cit.*, pp. 348–349.

[12]Margaret Mead, "A Redefinition of Education," in Alfred Lightfoot, ed., *Inquiries into the Social Boundaries of Education*. Chicago: Rand McNally and Company, 1972, p. 71.

2
World History: Its Aims and Objectives

At the signal starting the period, the class rapidly comes to order. Ms. Field's practiced eye sweeps the room, noting the absentees and reproving those few students who continue talking. With silence achieved, the teacher begins her lesson. "It seems that almost every week we read of a revolution somewhere in the world. There was the Cuban Revolution, revolutions in Vietnam and Iraq, and governments were overthrown in Honduras and the Dominican Republic. In fact, we are told that we live in revolutionary times. How can we tell whether a revolution has been successful?" She pauses for a moment, noting the different expressions on the faces before her. Slowly the hands go up.

Ms. Field: Johnny?

Johnny: We would have to figure out why the revolution occurred.

Marcia: If we knew what they hoped to gain—their aims—we would be able to tell.

Ms. Field: Good. Let's put that on the board. (*Under the heading "Criteria of Successful Revolution," Ms. Field writes: "1. Did it achieve its aims?" She turns back to the class to call on another volunteer.*)

Ann: A revolution is a serious thing. We would want to know if the results were lasting.

Ms. Field: Good. (*She adds: "2. Were its reforms lasting?" to the list.*)

Martin: It would be a good idea to know who led the revolution.

Walter: That doesn't seem important to me. What difference does it make who leads a revolution if it is successful? More important would be to know whether the revolution had much influence.

Agnes: We are not concerned here with leadership and reasons for immediate success. I agree with Ann; a revolution is a serious thing and it seems to me that, as Walter said, a successful revolution in the long run is one that has wide influence.

Ms. Field: I think we have to agree with Agnes. Over a long period of time, it is relatively unimportant who leads the revolution. I believe what most of you are getting at is the influence of the ideas of the revolution as a test of its success. (*She adds: "3. Did it have wide influence?" to the criteria listed on the board*.) Now in view of these criteria and the assignment you had for today, what problem do you think we should be concerned with today?

David: Was the French Revolution a success?

Ms. Field, noting that the forest of hands has subsided, nods and writes on the board: "Aim: Was the French Revolution a success?"

In the interchange above, Ms. Field elicited from the class the aim for the day's lesson: to evaluate the success of the French Revolution of 1789. In order to do so, the class will determine the criteria by which the success of the French or of any other revolution could be measured, and, by comparing what happened during and after the French Revolution with those criteria, reach at least a tentative conclusion.

Approaching the teaching of world history in this way serves many purposes. It encourages students to think about what they are doing and why they are doing it. It requires both teacher and class to examine the aim of the day in the light of the overarching outcomes expected from the study of social studies generally and of world history in particular. Last, but not least, it provides a means by which each instructional opportunity becomes three-dimensional in nature by attempting to develop knowledge, skills, and attitudes which are significant for an understanding of world history. It is to an examination of these aspects of the aims of teaching world history that this chapter is devoted.

Aims of Teaching World History

Although still the queen of the social studies, history is not so central to the curriculum as it once was. Because other disciplines have gained in ascendancy, history reigns but does not rule. On the other hand, because it has become broader in outlook and perspective than it once was, it remains, in the minds of many, the first among equals in the social studies sequence.

History has passed through two curriculum metamorphoses. Even a casual examination of the offerings in the social studies curriculum since 1900 reveals that the narrow requirement that students study ancient, medieval, and English history was expanded to include the study of European history, Western history, and world affairs. More importantly, the entire concept of what history is has likewise changed, so that today by the study of history we mean the study of social and economic growth or lack thereof as well as political development. We are concerned with the arts of peace as well as with the techniques of war. We are absorbed with the progress of science and technology and with the evolution of art, music, literature, education, and religion. The study of history involves the analysis of extraordinary movements and events in terms of their effects on the lives of ordinary men and women. Whereas history was once conceived as something static and unchanging, today it is constantly being reinterpreted.

That Clio has shorn herself of her rather Spartan fare made up almost exclusively of political and military affairs, and has embraced a much richer diet drawing on the concepts of world culture and civilization, is not a sudden development. It may be seen in the writings of Voltaire and von Ranke. Voltaire, in the introduction to his *The Age of Louis XIV*, explains, "It is not solely the life of Louis XIV that is here to be depicted. A greater object is in view, which is to depict for posterity not the actions of a single man, but the minds of men in the most enlightened century that ever was." Voltaire cautions that readers will not read exhaustive details of wars, battles, or treaties since "not everything that is done deserved recording." Instead, "only that which merits the attention of the ages will be dealt with—that which depicts the genius and manners of men, or which serves to instruct and inculcate the love of country, of virtue and of art."[1]

In the writings of Leopold von Ranke we may find still another plea for a broadening of the perspective in which history is viewed. Although von Ranke urged that historians attempt to write history as it "actually happened," it was he who encouraged the concept of universal history. However, because of his insistence on critical analysis of original sources and on the reconstruction of what happened based on these sources, his disciples often took a too narrow view of his historical approach. They forgot that, in addition to his encouragement of the development of particular details, he urged that historians must fashion a "universal view" and must lift their sights from the exclusive observation and investigation of detail. "Those historians are also mistaken," he

[1]François Marie Arouet (Voltaire), "Letter to Jean Baptiste Dubos," in Fritz Stern, ed., *The Varieties of History*. New York: Meridian Books, 1956, pp. 40, 43.

said, "who consider history simply an immense aggregate of particular facts, which it behooves one to commit to memory."[2]

What are the implications of these statements for the aims of world history instruction? Surely, teachers of history could do worse than to use Voltaire's criteria for the writing of history for their teaching of it. The aims that Voltaire sought to achieve in writing *The Age of Louis XIV* lend themselves admirably as criteria by which teachers of world history might select the content of their course. Voltaire suggests that, to be effective, history must depict the genius as well as the manners of people. Voltaire urges that history might be used to instruct and to encourage the love of country. In world history, we must add to love of country a love of humanity as well. And where Voltaire urges that history inculcate love of virtue and of art, we can add—without violating or distorting the views of Voltaire—the virtues of intellectual honesty and of open-mindedness, of racial and religious tolerance, and of the art of effective participation in world affairs.

History teachers should listen to the historian who warns against making history simply an immense aggregate of particular facts. History does have "facts," of course; and students are expected to know them and study them. But along with von Ranke, teachers must seek and fashion with their classes a "universal view" that encourages synthesis as well as analysis in the study of the relationships between causes and effects, people and nations, events and geography, economy and resources. In the hands of a skillful history teacher, history becomes, in Macaulay's words, "philosophy teaching by example."

In his essay "History" in *The Social Studies and the Social Sciences*, Joseph R. Strayer writes: "Study of civilizations that are remote in space and time increases the understanding of human behavior and promotes the desired attitude of tolerance and respect for human achievement of any kind."[3] The study of world history may be said to contribute to (1) an understanding of human behavior; (2) a respect for human

achievement; and (3) a background for civic competence. The study of world history has as its highest order of priority the development of an awareness of the inhumanity of men and women to one another and a keen appreciation of our responsibility for one another. In essence, the central theme in world history must be an affirmative answer to Cain's sullen query, "Am I my brother's keeper?"

Getting Started

When planning to achieve a three-dimensional quality, the world history teacher must ask, "What selection of subject matter will best facilitate understanding?" "What methodology and instructional materials will demonstrate the skills of the historian or the skills required for effective world citizenship?" "What questions will best impale the class on the horns of a dilemma out of which will develop an appreciation of the ties that make a community of nations possible?"

How one starts the lesson will make a great deal of difference in how the lesson will develop and what its outcomes are likely to be. To the extent possible, each day's lesson should start with something with which to "catch the conscience" of the students or to arouse and hold the students' interest. This is no easy task. However, some imagination, a deep knowledge of history, and understanding of what motivates students will help teachers frame good starting questions. Some suggestions follow:

1. **Relating Past and Present:** "The exploration and discovery of the New World has been described as being just as exciting and just as ambitious an undertaking as the discovery and explorations now going on in outer space. To what extent do you agree or disagree?"

2. **Using a Cartoon:** "How would you interpret the cartoon? To what extent would you agree or disagree with it?" (Stick figures quickly drawn on the board while the class watches and perhaps laughs is an age-old but forgotten device to hold the students' interest. It has a thousand uses; it need not be perfect; and a little practice can sharpen skills considerably.)

---

[2]Leopold von Ranke, "The Ideal of Universal History," in *op. cit.*, p. 59.

[3]New York: Harcourt Brace and World, 1962, p. 35.

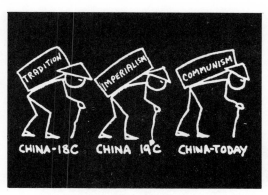

China's Tragic History

3. **Using a Poem:** For a lesson on the problems growing out of the Industrial Revolution, have the class interpret the following lines from Sara Cleghorn:

> The golf links lie so near the mill
> That almost every day
> The laboring children can look out
> And see the men at play.

4. **Outrageous (but Accurate) Statements: Mussolini:** "When I hear the word liberty, I reach for my gun." How do you explain Mussolini's point of view? Or, why did he make the remark?

5. **For the Study of History:** "History is bunk." Would you agree or disagree? Why? Or, "History is lies people have agreed upon." Would you agree or disagree? Why?

6. **Dramatic Episode:** Do something dramatic (e.g., knock over a globe, throw an eraser across the room, pick a "fight" with a student) and ask students to reconstruct "what happened." How do you explain the different versions of what took place? How can we reconstruct what actually took place? What problems for the historian does this suggest?

7. **Using Chronology:** Draw a chalkline on the board. Ask students to come to the chalkboard and identify that segment of time which represents all of humankind's existence on earth, and that segment which represents all of modern times since, say, 1500. Students will be astounded to see that all of humankind's time on earth as a segment of the chalkline can hardly be seen from the rear of the room; while the segment on modern times can scarcely be seen by anyone except the person at the board. When we study history, we study but a moment in time. Would you agree or disagree? Why?

8. **Role Playing:** Pretend you are one of the following: housewife, working woman, soldier, diplomat, factory worker, officer, munitions maker. How would you feel about the newspaper headline that declared "Austria Declares War on Serbia"?

9. **Imaginary Letter:** Slowly open an envelope or unfold a sheet of paper. "The other day I received a letter I would like to read to you. 'I hear you are going to discuss the glorious achievements of the Soviet Union. I hope you will tell them of the great and good democracy the Soviet Union is. Your friend: Brezhnev.' If you had received such a letter how would you answer your 'friend' "?

Most skilled world history teachers prefer to have the aim elicited from the class through the use of one or more of the approaches suggested above. The aim should be written on the board and framed as a question. When framed as an appropriate question, it contributes to the three-dimensional quality of effective world history teaching. An aim which is presented to the class as "To show how the French Revolution came to France" may be satisfactory, and a reasonably good lesson may flow from it. But how much better is the aim Ms. Field elicited, "Was the French Revolution a success?" Other probing, three-dimensional aims for such a lesson are possible. For example, "Did the French Revolution bring revolution to the world?" may be the aim out of which a deeply satisfying lesson may also evolve. An aim such as this may sound overly ambitious, and with some groups it may well be more than the class can absorb. Nevertheless, we believe with Robert Browning, who said, ". . .a man's reach should exceed his grasp, Or what's a heaven for?" The nature of world history demands that our aims exceed our grasp if we are to exploit the limitless opportunities world history provides—and if we are to help prepare the way for a world in which, using Tennyson's words, "the war drum throbbed no longer and the battle flags were furled in the Parliament of Man, the Federation of the World."

3
World History: Curriculum Patterns

Having taken the attendance, checked the previous day's homework, and given the advance assignment, Mr. Vance directs the attention of the group to his neatly drawn board diagram.

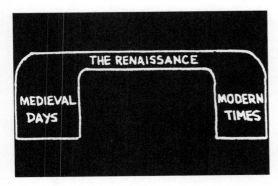

Mr. Vance: Do you agree or disagree with the thought expressed in the drawing on the board? Ephram?

Ephram: I agree with it because during the Renaissance modern ideas that we have today began.

Mr. Vance: How do the rest of you feel? Rose?

Rose: Well, I don't see that the diagram says very much; it just shows the Renaissance joining medieval and modern days.

Estelle: That's just it. It shows the Renaissance bridging the period between medieval days and our own days.

Howard: If that's what the diagram shows I don't agree with it. Medieval days started as far back as the fifth century, about the time of the fall of Rome, and they stopped around the middle of the fifteenth century, I think. What happened to the thousand years in between? Weren't they a bridge to modern times?

Mr. Vance: Perhaps they were a bridge from Roman days to the Renaissance.

Lou: That's not right. The Renaissance ended about the fifteenth century and you can't call that modern, can you?

Mr. Vance: You cannot call it modern if by modern you mean what happened just yesterday. But in the thousands of years of recorded history, the most recent five hundred years or so are generally called the modern era, and its history is called modern history.

Julia: According to the diagram, then, the Renaissance was a bridge or transition from medieval to modern times because it came in between these two eras?

Mr. Vance: That's right. What questions, then, might we raise in view of Julia's explanation of

15

the board diagram?

Eli: One question is "Why has the Renaissance been called a bridge to modern times?"

During the remainder of the lesson, Mr. Vance struggled to elicit from the class the meaning and implications of the Renaissance. He sought to have the class identify those characteristics of modern times that were beginning to emerge, such as the growth of national states and the beginning of national languages, the reluctance to accept authority as the sole source of knowledge and a willingness to experiment, a gradual decline in superstition and in the all-pervasive influence of religion, the growth of interest in secular affairs, including commerce and industry, as well as a concern for the artistic and technological.

When the lesson was brought to an abrupt close by the bell, Mr. Vance felt a sense of frustration, rather than of satisfaction. His lesson had not gone well, and most of the concepts he had sought so desperately to make concrete remained vague. Most students seemed to have but a nebulous notion of the chronological sequence of the intervals of time being compared. Moreover, the vacant, expressionless faces, the blank looks that met his eye as the students left for their next class, served notice that the daily dosage of world history he had been so diligently preparing, so conscientiously teaching, and so assiduously assigning was having but fleeting effects in terms of accomplishing the aims for which the course in world history had been created.

In the selection above, the teacher tried, with but limited success, to elicit a useful aim for a lesson on the Renaissance which he hoped would be three-dimensional in nature. He tried, through the diagram and questioning, for a lesson that would contribute to a better understanding of the Renaissance, some skill in interpreting a diagram, and some appreciation of the fact that modern times, as we know them, may be said to have been born during the Renaissance.

Studying the Renaissance in this way is both useful and appropriate, but why study the Renaissance at all? What is the relationship between the scholarly content of world history and world history as a high school course of study?

There have been few, if any, better explanations of the appropriate relationship between subject matter as understood by the advanced scholar and as it is viewed by the learner than the following statement by John Dewey. Written in *Democracy and Education* more than sixty years ago, it is a paragraph which gains in relevance as it mellows with age:

From the standpoint of the educator. . . the various studies represent working resources, available capital. Their remoteness from the experience of the young is. . .real. The subject matter of the learner is not, therefore. . .identical with the formulated, the crystallized, and yet systematized subject matter of the adult; the material as found in books and in works of art. The latter represents the *possibilities* of the former; not its existing state. It enters directly into the activities of the expert and the educator, not into that of the beginner, the learner. Failure to bear in mind the difference in subject matter from the respective standpoints of teacher and student is responsible for most of the mistakes made in the use of texts and other expressions of pre-existent knowledge. . . .

To the one who is learned, subject matter is extensive, accurately defined, and logically interrelated. To the one who is learning, it is fluid, partial, and connected through his personal occupations. The problem of teaching is to keep the experience of the student moving in the direction of what the expert already knows. Hence the need that the teacher know both subject matter and the characteristic needs and capacities of the student. . . .[1]

According to this view the teacher requires a substantial fund of scholarship—a well-rounded and penetrating insight into the totality of forces that make up the subject known as world history. In framing the course of study in world history, the teacher's responsibility is to develop so profound a view of scholarship as to be in a position to pick and choose what will be taught and what will be left out.

Choosing what to leave out is the hardest task before the teacher of world history. The "courage of omission" may be said to be one of the qualities which the world history teacher must develop. Most teachers of world history try to teach too much. Little wonder. There is so much to be taught. It is the task of the teacher, working within the guidelines of structured curriculum bulletins and instructional guides, to furnish those boundaries. With a well-formulated concept of world history, the world history teacher can then selectively identify those topics which best lend themselves to an understanding of the world community in which we all live.

[1] John Dewey, *Democracy and Education*. New York: The Macmillan Company, 1916, pp. 214–215.

Sources of Dissatisfaction with the World History Course of Study

The sources of dissatisfaction with the world history course are many and are of long duration. James Bryant Conant, almost twenty years ago, pointed to the widespread dissatisfaction with the world history course.[2] Among the many sources of discontent, the following points are perhaps among the more significant:

1. **Despite a change in name, much of what passes for world history remains European-centered or, at best, Western-oriented.** "This Europocentric fallacy still distorts our concepts of the past despite the pressure to achieve a still more balanced, a more global interpretation."[3]

2. **World history courses today continue to neglect such cultural areas as Latin America, Africa, and East Asia.** These cultural areas, when they are studied at all, are often treated merely as offshoots of European history; and the primitive culture of the "natives" is placed in juxtaposition to the more cultivated ways and manners of Europeans. The alleged inferiority of other people, when not patently stated as such, is implied through failure to deal with the non-Western world on its own terms.

3. **World history courses have been overly concerned with political affairs and inadequately concerned with cultural, scientific, or technological developments.** As a result, world history has taken

[2] James B. Conant, *The American High School Today*. New York: McGraw-Hill Book Company, 1959, p. 42.

[3] Geoffrey Bruun, "Western Civilization," in Harold C. Hunt, ed., *High School Social Studies Perspectives*. Boston: Houghton Mifflin Company, 1962, p. 152.

the form of emphasis on struggles for power among the mighty and has failed to note "the short and simple annals of the poor" and the peaceful progress of humankind.

4. **These three limitations of the curriculum grow in part out of inadequate time allotment.** A year's course in world history must be highly selective, and in such a short period of time students can neither learn the structure of a discipline, nor obtain adequate insights or background for an understanding of today's world problems.

5. **Aggravating these difficulties is the question of where in the social studies curriculum world history should be offered.** Currently, world history is most often given in the tenth grade. It is questionable, however, whether high school sophomores are ready for the more difficult concepts of world history: nationalism, imperialism, democracy, industrialism. Besides being complex, these concepts change meaning and vary subtly and sometimes starkly, according to who uses them and the context in which they are used.

6. **The materials for the world history course have likewise been a source of longstanding grievance.** Much of the reading material shares the European myopia common to the course itself. A great deal of it is written at levels far too advanced for the high school sophomore.

7. **Teacher limitations are likewise a problem in attempting to offer a good world history course.** Although many teachers would like to break away from the European orientation of the course, they are unable to do so because of their own inadequacies in non-Western culture and civilization. They lack the scholarship and the insight to select those people, events, great movements, or illustrative moments of history which best promote a universal view.

The World History Course of Study: Patterns of Organization

There are a number of basic patterns of organization in the world history course of study. The more important of these follow:

World History as Chronology: History is nothing if it is not chronology. That is, what makes history distinctive as a discipline is that events are important because

they took place at a particular time. Chronology is essential to history, and the teaching of history cannot do without chronology. Because of the importance of chronology to history, for many years history was organized almost exclusively by dates. That is, one began, in effect, at the beginning, and year by year studied the events—mostly wars, revolutions, and political upheavals—that took place in any year. Important as chronology is, however, to organize a world history course exclusively upon chronology is probably a mistake. What students must learn and what teachers must teach is the interrelationship among events and some of the ways in which causes and effects are related to one another. Chronology may contribute to such understanding, but by itself it cannot do so.

The Topical Approach: Perhaps the next most important approach to the study of world history is its organization by topics. Thus, such topics as revolution, war, peace, industrial progress, imperialism, nationalism, to mention but a few, are discussed with a view toward identifying similarities and differences among events which appear to have certain elements in common. Thus, under revolution, the American, French, and Russian revolutions may be studied under a single unit of instruction, even though they took place at very different periods of time. Similarly, dictatorship may be studied by comparing the dictatorship, say, of Cromwell with that of recent dictators such as Hitler, Mussolini, Stalin, or Franco. Or absolute monarchies may be studied by comparing the monarchies of ancient Egypt with that of England under William the Conqueror, Henry VIII, or Elizabeth. These, in turn, may be compared with absolute monarchies as represented by, say, Peter or Catherine the Great in Russia. Moreover, both absolutism and dictatorship may both be compared to their counterparts in India, China, Africa, or Japan. This approach has much to recommend its use; nevertheless, if it ignores chronology its usefulness is very limited.

The Topical/Chronological Approach: This is probably the most frequently used form of organization and may be said to be the most traditional among the modern approaches to the study of world history.

While subjects are taught by topic—war, revolution, absolutism, dictatorship, democracy, nationalism, imperialism—these subjects are arranged in such a fashion that the student comes away with an understanding of the role that chronology plays. Because this is a relatively widely used form of organization, we provide in the next chapter a more detailed example of one possible internal organization.

World History as an Area Study: Among the faults found with most courses in world history is that they remain, even after all these many years in which teachers and historians have been urging the contrary, essentially centered on Western Europe. Other areas of the world are forced into the mold of ancient, medieval, and modern history, terms peculiarly appropriate for Western history, but not especially useful in the study of non-Western civilizations and cultures.

As a result, there are some, such as Leften Stavrianos and Ethel Ewing, who have urged that world history be organized by geographic areas. Ethel Ewing suggests the following areas: Far Eastern Society, India and Southeast Asia, the Middle East and Moslem Society, Latin American Society. Stavrianos suggests the following areas: The United States, the Soviet Union, Latin America, the Middle East, India, China, sub-Saharan Africa. With the area study approach, it is possible to integrate rather effectively other disciplines which make up the social sciences. Thus, the geographic, political, economic, as well as historical forces which shaped the development of those regions, may be brought together into an interesting and revealing mosaic. Moreover, under such a form of organization, the non-Western regions appear to get fairer treatment.

Although this approach has much to commend it, it is not altogether satisfactory. Because it depends upon specific geographic regions, one may not always find cultural unity among the nations of the area. While Israel, for example, is in the Middle East, its history is quite different from that of its Arab neighbors. Japan, while part of east Asia, during the past one hundred years has followed political and economic developments not unlike those of the West. To study Japan only in the East Asian context may be a mistake.

In the area study, history may often be neglected, as the approach is essentially interdisciplinary, drawing on geography, sociology, and anthropology as well as history. While this may be desirable, chronology as well as a unified world-wide theme placed in historical perspective may be lost. Another point that area study raises is that it suggests, or appears to suggest, that each area of the world deserves equal attention. In an absolute sense, perhaps they do; but if we are to follow the dictum in this chapter—that the teacher must have the courage of omission, since the time allocated to world history is finite while the subject matter is infinite—some selection of emphases must be made.

History as Inquiry: This approach to the study of world history appears to have crested after having enjoyed a very considerable popularity for about a decade. With a philosophical rationale provided by the psychologist Jerome Bruner and a curriculum and methodology provided mostly by Edwin Fenton of Carnegie-Mellon University, the inquiry approach to teaching world history suggests that what is important is not the subject matter but rather the tools by which historians determine what actually happened. Students, according to this view, must be encouraged to pursue their own inquiry given basic data and/or documents, and they are to discover for themselves the basic facts of what took place and why. Using appropriate artifacts (models, etc.), students become their own historians and learn to generalize, to subject a document to internal and external criticism, and otherwise to handle original data in such a way as to discover history for themselves.

This approach has had wide vogue and has left an indelible imprint on the teaching of world history. Nevertheless, several criticisms may be suggested. For one thing, good materials are not readily available. When available, they take considerable skill in using. The approach relies almost exclusively on induction (going from the specific to the general) and largely ignores deduction (going from the general to the specific). Moreover, there is some question as to the desirability of making historians out of students who are not going to be historians. In addition, what if they "discover," through their own devices, that which is inaccurate or contrary to what actually took place? To force them to reach the "correct" conclusion is inconsistent with inquiry approaches.[4]

As in area studies, the inquiry approach tends to minimize history and to enthrone anthropology and sociology. Indeed one approach which has had considerable development and publicity is called *Man: A Course of Study*. This approach, largely anthropological in nature, was developed by the Education Development Center and has had the support of Jerome Bruner and a number of other prominent psychologists and sociologists. While historians of note have been involved in this project, history is not much in evidence.

These, in summary, may be said to be the major forms of curriculum organization in world history. There are, however, a variety of other possibilities. For example, history may be organized around the study of great men and women. Thomas Carlyle thought this approach to be best. He said, "In all epochs of the world's history, we shall find the Great Man to have been the indispensable saviour of his epoch; the lightning without which the fuel never would have burnt. The History of the World. . .was the Biography of Great Men."[5]

Other approaches involve treating major topics in depth (so called post-holing). This structure makes it possible for students to become deeply acquainted with a few topics, but runs the risk of denying to them an understanding of the all-encompassing scope of world history. Still another form of organization of a world history course is around great documents. Thus, world history may be taught by examining great documents such as the Magna Carta (1215), or the Declaration of the Rights of Man (1789), or through speeches made by Bismarck, Gandhi, Nyrere, or Chou En-lai, to mention but a few possibilities. Although

such a course can be effective in contributing to the aims of world history, it probably requires a superior student body to begin with and superior teachers and teaching as well. Carefully used by skilled teachers, it is a useful approach.

World History as Current Events, Contemporary Affairs, and Controversial Issues

In addition to dealing with the vast scope and content of world history, the teacher must always plan to deal with meaningful current events, contemporary affairs, and controversial issues.

A controversial issue has been defined as a "problem on which there are honest differences of opinion." World history is filled with controversial issues; they have a vital place in the course of study. They often motivate discussion and arouse interest. They show that the problems of the world have yet to be solved and that the students have a responsibility in solving them. Controversial issues in the world history class are so important and unavoidable that the following suggestions are made as a guide to their use:

1. **The controversial issue chosen for discussion must be within the scope of the intellectual ability of the class.**

2. **Some issues are not controversial and should not be presented as such.** The virtue of peace over war, or democracy over dictatorship are examples of these.

3. **In dealing with controversial issues, students should be encouraged to formulate their own views and support them with evidence.** Most controversial issues have no immediate solution; it is important, however, that students learn some of the techniques by which data are gathered and how compromise is achieved.

No course in world history would be complete without adequate consideration of current affairs,[6] "history in the making." So overpowering, however, are the current affairs of our day that, unless care is taken,

---

[4]These criticisms are based on Gerald Leinwand, "Queries on Inquiry in the Social Studies," *Social Education*. Volume XXX, No. 6, October, 1966, pp. 412–414.

[5]Thomas Carlyle, "On Heroes, Hero-Worship, and the Heroic in History," in Fritz Stern, ed., *The Varieties of History*. New York: Meridian Books, 1956, p. 103.

[6]Sometimes a distinction is made between current affairs and current events. The latter is usually a single significant episode (e.g., an earthquake in Romania). The former is a subject that has aroused sustained interest by the mass media (e.g., amnesty for Vietnam deserters).

the world history course may become only a course in current affairs, not history. To keep current affairs in place and in perspective, the following suggestions are made:

1. **Use current affairs to introduce a lesson.** This often serves as a good discussion motivator and enables students to relate the past to the present.

2. **A current affairs lesson should be devoted to a *single* significant topic, rather than to a series of unrelated reports.**

3. **Students should be encouraged to cut out and summarize newspaper articles which relate to topics already studied and to paste them in their notebooks.**

· 4. **Homework assignments can be enriched by calling attention to appropriate newspaper articles and radio and TV programs.**

A Do-It-Yourself World History Course of Study

Curriculum, by definition, may be said to be all the activities that a school provides to further the education of children. This means that the teacher is the school's chief curriculum maker. In no other area is this more justified than in the area of world history. Teachers choose the emphasis they wish to give and the procedures and activities they wish to undertake in furthering the aims of world history instruction. Curriculum bulletins and course outlines may serve as guides, make suggestions, and map out the terrain over which the teacher may take world history students. But if curriculum bulletins propose, teachers dispose. It is the teacher as skillful tactician who chooses specific subject matter, procedures, and materials to determine the world history course of study that is actually followed.

As a result, teachers are urged to develop their own world history courses of study, drawing on their own scholarship, the needs of their students, the guidelines provided by the various curriculum bulletins that they may have available to them, and their understanding of the emerging currents in today's world. The approach is eclectic, requiring the teacher to set his or her own boundaries to the course of study to be offered, while exercising great courage in leaving out that which does not appear to be appropriate.

A few guidelines for what may be called a "do-it-yourself curriculum" may help teachers to decide upon an effective world history curriculum appropriate for their students and the times in which they live:

1. **In selecting the topics to be considered in world history, there should be diversity of time and space.** That is, the content should draw on ancient and modern history and should attempt to deal with Western and non-Western society.

2. **A study of nineteenth and twentieth century developments is required if students are to understand some of the roots of current problems, such as several problems in China, Eastern Europe, and Southeast Asia.**

3. **The teacher should select a few areas or eras and study them in some detail.** This may sacrifice a measure of continuity which, to be sure, is desirable in any course which purports to be history; but in choosing to deal with certain topics in detail, we are placing emphasis on scholarship rather than on superficiality. A few well delivered lectures during the course of a year may be used to furnish the required continuity.

A do-it-yourself approach to the development of a world history course of study is not a haphazard undertaking. Nor does it suggest that curriculum bulletins and related publications be ignored or overlooked. What it does suggest is that each year's course of study must be tailored anew to the needs of the students the world history teacher is then teaching and to the requirements of events of the day. These factors have an inevitable impact on what will be chosen for class discussion, what amount of time will be devoted to it, what procedures will be used, what questions will be framed, and what materials of instruction will be required.

4

World History and the Socratic Method

"And it seems to me, in spite of what Wanda said, that there is no question about his being a dictator. He runs the Soviet government, doesn't he? Look at the Berlin Wall if you want more proof." The class listens as Joe finishes his contribution to the discussion. As he sits down, Mr. D'Angelo, satisfied with the responses he has been getting during a lesson comparing fascism and communism, but dissatisfied with the logic of the statement he has just heard, probes for greater accuracy and enlightenment.

Mr. D'Angelo: How does the Berlin Wall prove that the Soviet leader is a dictator?

Terry: I was wondering about Joe's reasoning. What does the Berlin Wall have to do with the question of whether he is a dictator? It has no more to do with it than our sending aid to India proves that we're a democracy. Our text says that the Communist Party runs the Soviet government and that its head is the head of the Communist Party in Russia. Therefore, he must run the Soviet government.

John: I agree with Terry. Not only is the Premier a dictator but he has the military backing he needs. The May Day pictures of the Red Army show a well fed and well equipped force.

Mr. D'Angelo: If the Premier is a dictator, why should he worry about the success or failure of his agricultural program? Fred?

Fred: He must be afraid of the people, afraid of revolution. All dictators are. That's the only way to get rid of them.

Amy: I'm sure Fred remembers, though, that after Stalin's death, there were several peaceful changes in leadership—Bulganin, Malenkov—

without revolution. Apparently, changes can be made from within. The Soviet Premier must be worried about agricultural success or failure because he is worried about his standing within the Communist Party. If his policies do not work out he may be replaced by someone else. It looks as if he needs the support of other leaders of the Party.

Carol: Didn't Mr. D'Angelo tell us yesterday of the interlocking arrangement between the Communist Party's Presidium and the Soviet government's Council of Ministers? I also read for my book report *Two Ways of Life* by William Ebenstein. It said that the small group of men who make up the Communist Party's Presidium are the real source of power in the Soviet Union. If that is so, then the Premier must satisfy those men. I heard once that within the Presidium there is complete freedom of debate and expression and that there are hot debates on policies for the party and the country. Votes are taken and the majority rules. But once a policy is adopted, that's the end of debate; public criticism by any member of the Presidium is forbidden.

Mr. D'Angelo: That was a fine contribution, Carol. You mentioned the Princeton scholar, William Ebenstein. In his book *Today's Isms*, Mr. Ebenstein says, "The quarrel between communism and fascism results from the inability of burglars to agree over the division of the loot, whereas the quarrel between communism and democracy is that between the burglar and the law."[1] To what extent do you agree or disagree?

---

[1] William Ebenstein, *Today's Isms*. Englewood Cliffs, New Jersey: Prentice-Hall, 1959, p. 113.

The Role of Questioning in Teaching World History

Because to question well is to teach well, teachers generally, and world history teachers especially, need to master the art of skillful questioning. The use of the question for didactic purposes is called the Socratic method. In the excerpt that follows, Socrates elicited from an illiterate slave the correct geometric principle that a square constructed on the diagonal of a given square would be double the size of the original one. Socrates, as is well known, questioned the values by which Athenians then lived and was sentenced to take poison for his pains. No similar fate awaits the world history teacher who chooses to use the Socratic method. We acknowledge, however, that to use questions to probe for understanding, to reenforce for mastery, and to encourage continued questioning by our students is a dangerous way to teach. It is, nevertheless, a rewarding one that is well worth the risk.

Socrates: Now, my boy, tell me: Do you know that a four-cornered space is like this?
Boy: I do.
Socrates: Is this a four-cornered space having these lines equal, all four?
Boy: Surely.
Socrates: And these across the middle, are they not equal too?
Boy: Oh yes.
Socrates: Then if this side is two feet long and this two, how many feet would the whole be? Or look at it this way: if it were two feet this way, and only one the other, would not the space be once two feet?
Boy: Yes.
Socrates: But as it is two feet this way also, isn't it twice two feet?
Boy: Yes, so it is.
Socrates: Then how many are twice two feet? Count and tell me.

Boy: Four, Socrates.
Socrates: Well, could there be another such space twice as big, but of the same shape, with all the lines equal like this one?
Boy: Yes.
Socrates: How many feet will there be in that, then?
Boy: Eight.
Socrates: Very well, now try to tell me how long will be each line of that one. The line of this one is two feet; how long would the line of the double one be?
Boy: The line would be double, Socrates, that is clear.
Socrates (aside to Menon): You see, Menon, that I am not teaching this boy anything; I ask him everything. . . .[2]

Socrates was, of course, teaching. Every question was designed to help the child solve the problem for himself. The boy was led step by step, in a clear sequence, from simpler to more complex ideas. Moreover, the learner was actively involved in the learning process in that in the process of discovering the solution for himself he always had to respond. Socrates was continually alert to the boy's progress. At a later point in the dialogue, when the boy says, "I don't understand," Socrates prompts him, gives him clues, and reminds him of what he already knows. Although Socrates himself denied that he told the boy anything, many or most of the questions actually impart information even as they elicit it.

"Knowledge," according to Socrates, "will not come from teaching but from questioning."[3] Socrates knew that in the skillful use of the question, more than in anything else, lay the fine art of teaching. The ques-

[2]W. H. D. Rouse, translator, *Great Dialogues of Plato: Meno.* New York: The New American Library, Mentor Books, 1956, pp. 43–44.
[3]*Ibid.*, p. 50.

tion is the universal implement of good teaching, applicable to all ages and suitable to all stages of instruction, whether in the one-to-one relationship of one Socrates to one boy or in the more usual relationship in the schools of today of one teacher to thirty or more pupils.

Merely asking questions in and of itself does not ensure effective teaching of world history. Since our aims are three-dimensional, and since the world history class must be a microcosm of democratic practice and a laboratory in which the skills and tools necessary for understanding the work of the social scientist can be developed, the kind of questions we ask will determine the nature of the responses we receive and the extent to which our aims are being achieved. It is upon the artistry of the teacher's questioning that success in world history teaching depends.

By artistry in questioning we mean that through experience and scholarly competence, the teacher is able to use the question to achieve balance and harmony, unity and coherence, and emotional and intellectual equilibrium among the various elements of a lesson. Just as it is impossible to achieve artistry in playing the piano by "following these simple directions" or to become a great painter by "following the numbers," so it is impossible to achieve artistry in questioning by following any given set of directions. However, lessons that are artistic, in that more than technical competence or academic achievement is evident, have these characteristics:

1. **There is a subtle balance between so-called fact and thought questions.** That is, any lesson in which questions beginning with Who? What? When? or Where? predominate is likely to be an unar-

tistic and unharmonious one. These factual questions, vital though they may be, are but the building blocks upon which the implications of the lesson are built. To be content with a lesson that relies exclusively on such questions is to test rather than to teach, is to be satisfied with memorized responses, and is to revert to the days of the recitation when a student was expected merely to repeat what had been studied the night before.

2. **Students give sustained answers based on weighing and interpreting data as they see them.** Answers may be expressions of opinion supported by appropriate factual data; they may be reinterpretations of readings in the text or in related sources; they may be criticisms of public figures or of historical personages.

3. **Many students volunteer responses to a single question.** Thus, the last question Mr. D'Angelo raised (see p. 23) certainly provoked a variety of responses. Probably the brighter students would object to the rather glib generalization about the difference between communism and fascism. Others might agree or disagree in varying measure. As they give their answers, the teacher listens carefully, so that at precisely the right moment another student may be called upon or another question asked, each time relating one answer to another answer, one question to another question, or one question to an answer previously given. As the teacher listens, he or she is alert for evidence of glibness and superficiality and is careful to ask the next question only when sure that the groundwork has been carefully prepared.

4. **Non-volunteers are also drawn into the lesson.** As a result, during the usual forty-minute class session, most students,

perhaps two-thirds or more, should participate. A lesson dominated by a handful of students cannot be considered artistic, no matter how effective the questions or how carefully they are worded. Nor can a lesson dominated by the teacher be considered an artistic one. Once a well framed question has been asked, the teacher ideally should only have to recognize each student in turn and to encourage each to participate. Each participates, not only to respond to the teacher's question, but to comment on what other students have said, to make additions, modifications, corrections, or comments.

5. **The teacher must have a sense of the dramatic, achieved through timing, voice quality, and enthusiasm.** Asked at an inappropriate moment, with insufficient vigor and energy, without a dramatic pause to prepare the class to listen with anticipation, the best prepared question elicits but meager response. Conversely, not every question must be laboriously worked over before it is asked. Often the teacher's warmth and personality, the vibrancy of voice, and the tone established within the class enable the teacher to use a kind of oral shorthand in phrasing questions. Thus, some teachers can ask questions framed incorrectly according to the rules and yet elicit highly appropriate responses.

The comedian Jack Benny, true artist that he was, could get so many prolonged laughs out of his jokes that he was sparing in using up the material his writers provided. Similarly, the teacher of world history, true artist that he or she is, uses each question to optimum advantage in an artistic effort to have students identify data, evaluate evidence, reach conclusions, or suspend judgment until the data are all in. As with all art, much depends upon technical skills, which can be mastered with study and practical application.

Some Examples of Good Questions*

Comparison: How do the views of Begin differ from those of Sadat on achieving peace in the Middle East?

Contrast: How do you explain the fact that North Africa was part of the cradle of

*In many questions adding "Why?" or "Why not?" is implied.

civilization but sub-Saharan Africa was not?

Evaluation: Which has had a more profound effect on world history, Magellan's circumnavigation of the globe or the modern landing of men on the moon? Why?

Interpretation: What did Adam Smith mean when he wrote in *The Wealth of Nations* that "Every individual. . .is led. . .by an invisible hand."?

Proof: It has been said that the standard of living most people enjoyed was as high in 1850 B.C. in ancient Egypt as it was in Europe in 1850 A.D. Can this statement be substantiated?

Relationship: How will a bumper crop of wheat in the Soviet Union affect the price of bread in the world market?

Application: In view of the political characteristics of a democratic government, how would you evaluate the government of England in 1830?

Judgment: To what extent may it be said that America did not really "open Japan"; instead, the Japanese "came out"?

Criticism: Was the action of the United Nations in sending a "police force" into Korea justified? Why or why not?

Agreement: Would you agree or disagree with the statement that World War I was the war nobody won? Why or why not?

Personalized: If you were a member of the British Parliament in 1914, would you have voted for Home Rule for Ireland? Why or why not?

Some Examples of Poor Questions

Leading: Wouldn't you say Hitler was more a villain than Napoleon?

Chorus: "Who wrote the Communist Manifesto? Class?" (Questions that encourage one word answers will also encourage chorus answers.)

Whiplash: American neutrality in World War I helped which side?

Teacher-addressed: Can anyone tell me how to read a map scale?

Indefinite: How about South Vietnam's attitude toward Kissinger's efforts at negotiation?

Overlaid: What did the Boxers hope to accomplish in China, and what methods did they use?

Multiple: Who was responsible for the Atlantic Charter, and how successful was it?

Guessing: Was the League of Nations approved by the United States Senate?

Ambiguous: How does China differ from India?

Pupil-addressed: Mary, why was Sun Yat-sen unsuccessful in uniting China?

Reworded: How is a resolution adopted in the Security Council of the U.N.? How many votes are needed?

Repeated: How did Zaire become an independent country? How?

Numerous: To whom did the Congo belong? How were the Congolese treated? How did it get independence? Why does trouble persist?

Framing the World History Question

Mr. D'Angelo's lesson (see p. 23) was not only artistic, but his questioning was technically correct both in form and in execution. Good questions have the following characteristics:

1. **Effective questions indicate quite clearly what should be answered.** They are clear and definite in that they direct the attention of the students to a specific body of information upon which to draw for an answer.

2. **Good questions must be objective and unbiased.** Inquiry in world history requires the objective pursuit of truth. Nowhere must the world history teacher be more cautious than in framing questions so that they do not reveal personal preferences or impose value judgments on students. Words that color questions by casting overtones of bias should be avoided; yet, on occasion, many teachers are unconsciously guilty of such usage.

3. **A well framed question is vivid in that it tells something as well as asks something.** "How did Hitler gain power in Germany?" lacks color, imagination, or strength. The following is better: "William Shirer, in *The Rise and Fall of the Third Reich*, declared, 'The Germans imposed the Nazi tyranny on themselves.'[4] To what extent does Hitler's rise to power justify this conclusion?" The question introduced related literature and so brought enrichment to the lesson. By quoting directly from the

[4]William L. Shirer, *The Rise and Fall of the Third Reich*. New York: Simon and Schuster, 1960, p. 187.

book in class, the teacher makes the question immediate, vital, and vivid. By having the book in class and holding it up for the class to see as you quote from it, you add a sense of the dramatic, a quality so important in the teaching of any subject.

4. **The well framed question avoids a yes-no or other one-word answer.** "Did the Senate ratify the Versailles Treaty?" is worse than useless because it elicits but a single word, and it may give rise to chorus answering. To help teachers frame questions that avoid single word responses, we urge that they begin their question with "why?". The "why" question leads to many unsuspected avenues for further discussion. Well framed questions are tersely worded.

Asking Questions Properly and Handling Answers Effectively

Sometimes questions that meet all the criteria established for well framed questions fail to get the anticipated response. Factors of timing, of choice, of temperament may account for this. But beyond these factors there are techniques that will help teachers use a technically sound question to maximum advantage.

1. **Orient the questions to the group, rather than to the individual.** When teachers say "tell me," they are establishing a dialogue between them and an individual student. They are not asking the question for their benefit, but for the benefit of the class. They are not asking the question for the edification of an individual student, but to further the learning of the group. Thus, a question should always be addressed to the group as a whole. By doing this, everyone is drawn into the lesson and everyone can properly assume that he or she is expected to participate and to listen.

2. **Call upon students after the question is asked.** Just as the query "tell me" tends to shut the ears of other listeners, so prefacing your question by calling the student's name first effectively cuts off others who may have wanted to answer. Other members of the class assume, first, that they are not expected to answer even if they wanted to. Moreover, other members of the class may assume that they need not be

alert this time, because only one student has been asked to speak.

3. **Pause after asking a good question and before calling on a student.** A subtle pause serves notice to the members of the class that this is a good question that requires an extended answer, that it requires them to analyze what has been done in class to date, and perhaps to synthesize the components that have emerged from the lesson.

4. **Encourage students to address the class when speaking.** Because students usually face the teacher when answering questions, rather than the majority of the class, it is sound advice to move about the room from time to time and ask your questions from positions about the room as well as from the front desk. Thus, to force students sitting in the first seats to face the class, why not call on them from the rear of the room? Or why not call on students sitting near the window to respond to a question asked from the opposite side? Avoid, however, standing too near the window, since it forces students to gaze directly into the daylight and perhaps hurts their eyes.

5. **Avoid questions that call for guessing.** We have already pointed out that questions that call for one-word answers should be avoided, as should questions that encourage guessing. While spontaneous automatic guessing is to be discouraged, intuitive guessing has its uses. Jerome Bruner has this to say on the subject of guessing:

> Should students be encouraged to guess, in the interest of learning eventually how to make intelligent conjectures? Possibly there are certain kinds of situations where guessing is desirable and where it may facilitate the development of intuitive thinking to some degree. There may, indeed, be a kind of guessing that requires careful cultivation. Yet, in many classes in school, guessing is heavily penalized and is associated somehow with laziness. Certainly one would not like to educate students to do nothing but guess, for the guessing should always be followed up by as much verification and confirmation as necessary; but too stringent a penalty on guessing may restrain thinking of any sort and keep it plodding rather than permitting it to make occasional leaps.[5]

In handling student responses, the teacher must often play the devil's advocate and challenge the student to justify the answer. Students must be challenged to reevaluate their views, particularly some of their most cherished beliefs. Teachers should challenge students' value judgments by frequently asking: "Why did you say that?" "Do you agree or disagree? Why?" "If you believe such-and-such, then how can you believe so-and-so?" "Is such-and-such behavior (or belief) consistent with so-and-so behavior (or belief)?" "How do you explain that?"[6] Teachers need not always be the ones to do the challenging. Taking their cue from them, students will soon learn to listen for errors in logic, fallacies in conclusions, inconsistencies of statements, and errors of fact; soon this becomes the rhythm of the world history classroom.

And so the pace and rhythm of the world history lesson continues, forward to new work and to bright students, and backward for review and for the benefit of slower students. The teacher weaves in and out among the pupils to probe for the evidence of growth in knowledge, skills, and values. The voluble student is restrained with subtlety, the timid student is encouraged with kindness, the obdurate one is drawn into the discussion with firmness. Good teachers are not deceived by a constant show of hands eager to participate, because they may always be the hands of the same students. They consciously look to the rear of the room, to the "quiet corner," to the student who never seems to say anything, and test to see whether the answers of the students have been heard, appreciated, and absorbed.

In dealing with student responses it is imperative that a teacher remain alert to errors, omissions, inaccuracies, or inadequacies. Errors should be quickly and unobtrusively corrected if they are minor errors of fact (a date would usually fall into this category). Other shortcomings should be corrected by the class when possible. If vital information is omitted, the teacher should supply it if the class is unable to do so.

[5]Jerome Bruner, *The Process of Education*. New York: Alfred A. Knopf, Vintage Books, 1960, p. 64.

[6]Maurice P. Hunt and Lawrence E. Metcalf, *Teaching High School Social Studies*. New York: Harper and Brothers, 1955, p. 125.

Thus, a teacher asks a pivotal question, the response to which is essentially an evaluation of the most important provisions of the Fourteen Points, but the teacher finds that students are not discussing any of the significant ones. Rather than wait for someone to hit on it by chance, the teacher might ask, "Why was the Wilsonian principle of 'open covenants openly arrived at' (written on the board) a significant part of the Fourteen Points?" This prevents the pace of the lesson from flagging in the vain search for the one point that the teacher wants considered before the period ends.

The effective use of the question is largely the method of discovery. It enables students to discover for themselves "the generalization that lies behind a particular. . .operation." While Jerome Bruner said this of mathematics, it is equally true of world history. Socrates knew this in ancient Athens, and Jean Jacques Rousseau knew this in the latter part of the eighteenth century, as the following dialogue with Émile illustrates:

(Émile and Rousseau are lost in the woods— a predicament contrived by Rousseau to teach Émile the utility of geography.)

Jean Jacques: My dear Émile, what shall we do to get out?

Émile: I am sure I do not know. I am tired. I am hungry, I am thirsty. I cannot go any further.

Jean Jacques: Do you suppose I am any better off? I would cry too if I could make my breakfast off tears. Crying is no use, we must look about us. Let us see your watch; what time is it?

Émile: It is noon and I am so hungry!

Jean Jacques: Just so; it is noon and I am so hungry too.

Émile: You must be very hungry indeed.

Jean Jacques: Unluckily my dinner won't come to find me. It is twelve o'clock. This time yesterday we were observing the position of the forest from Montmorency. If only we could see the position of Montmorency from the forest.

Émile: But yesterday we could see the forest, and here we cannot see the town.

Jean Jacques: That is just it. If we could only find it without seeing it.

Émile: Oh! my dear friend!

Jean Jacques: Did not we say the forest was. . .

Émile: North of Montmorency.

Jean Jacques: Then Montmorency must lie. . .

Émile: South of the forest.

Jean Jacques: We know how to find north at midday.

Émile: Yes, by the direction of the shadows.

Jean Jacques: But the south?

Émile: What shall we do?

Jean Jacques: The south is opposite of north.

Émile: That is true; we need only to find the opposite of the shadows. That is the south! That is the south! Montmorency must be over there! Let us look for it there!

Jean Jacques: Perhaps you are right; let us follow this path through the wood.

Émile (clapping his hands): Oh, I can see Montmorency! There it is, quite plain, just in front of us! Come to luncheon, come to dinner, make haste! Astronomy [geography] is some use after all.[7]

The world history teacher could do worse than to follow in the footsteps of Socrates and Rousseau.

---

[7]From *Émile* by Jean Jacques Rousseau, translated by Barbara Foxley. An Everyman's Library Edition 1961, p. 144. Published in the United States by E. P. Dutton and reprinted with their permission.

The proclamation was sent to the Albany Relief Bazaar, in Jan., 1864, and brought to its funds $1,100, becoming the property of Gerrit Smith, Esq., who presented it to the United States Sanitary Commission, from whom it was purchased for $1,000 by vote of the New York Legislature, and is now in the State Library, at Albany.

5

World History and the Use of Sources

From her seat toward the rear of the room, Ms. Macdonald watches with some satisfaction a brief dramatization staged by members of this class in world history. This project is the culmination of a week of effort and after-school rehearsals. As Ms. Macdonald viewed it, the problem was to show the nature of industrial society as it emerged out of the so-called Industrial Revolution, and to do so not only in terms of impersonal forces (division of labor, the factory system, mass production) but insofar as it affected the ordinary men and women who were the victims as well as the beneficiaries of the new industrialization. But how to do it? How to reach students at an emotional as well as an intellectual level and in a limited amount of time?

Ms. Macdonald's scholarship came to her aid. She recalled that in 1833 a Parliamentary committee looked into the conditions of the labor of women and children in the factories of England. A bit of library research on her part located the documents, and the photocopier made it quite simple to copy a portion of testimony. Judicious adaptation to modernize the language, and to simplify it slightly, converted dry Parliamentary testimony into a script in which students could play the various roles. The dramatization based on this original source went as follows:

SCENE: *Three members of Parliament continue their hearings into the labor of women and children. They walk in and take their seats.*

First MP: The Committee on the Labor of Children will please come to order. (*Raps with the gavel.*) Call the first witness please.

Offstage voice: Will Mr. Coulson enter?

(**Mr. Coulson,** *poorly dressed, shuffles diffidently into the hearing chamber. He holds his cap awkwardly in his hands and abruptly sits down when invited to do so. The Members of Parliament begin their questioning.*)

First MP: How many children do you have, Mr. Coulson?

Coulson: I have three daughters, aged seven, ten and fourteen.

First MP: When did they start working in the mill?

Coulson: All three began to work at the age of six.

First MP: At what time in the morning during the busy season did your daughters go to the mills?

Coulson: During the busy season, for about six weeks, they went to work at three o'clock in the morning and worked until ten or nearly half past ten at night.

Second MP: What intervals were allowed for rest or refreshment during those nineteen hours of labor?

Coulson: They were given a quarter of an hour for breakfast and half an hour for dinner.

Second MP: Were they given supper?

Coulson: Oh, no, they were not.

Third MP: Was any of that time taken up in cleaning the machinery?

Coulson: They generally had to wipe the grease off. Sometimes this took the whole of the time at breakfast and then they had to get breakfast as they could.

First MP: Had you not great difficulty in awakening your children to this excessive labor?

Coulson: Yes, in the busy season we had to take them up asleep and shake them. Then we got them on the floor to dress them before we could get them off to their work; but not so during the regular season.

First MP: Supposing they had been late, what would have happened?

Coulson: They were quartered in the rush season as in the regular season.

Second MP: What do you mean by quartering?

Coulson: A quarter was taken off. That is, one fourth of their hourly salary was deducted.

Second MP: If they had been how much late?

Coulson: Five minutes.

Second MP: You mean if they were five minutes late, one quarter of their hourly salary would be withheld?

Coulson: Yes.

Third MP: What was the length of time they could be in bed during those busy days?

Coulson: It was near eleven o'clock before we could get them into bed after a little food, and then my wife used to stay up all night for fear that she could not get them ready for the morning. In general, me or my wife got up at two o'clock to dress them.

Second MP: So that they had not above four hours' sleep at this time?

Coulson: No, they had not.

First MP: For how long a period did this last?

Coulson: About six weeks it held; it was only done when they were very rushed. It was not often that.

First MP: The usual hours were from six in the morning till half past eight at night?

Coulson: Yes.

First MP: With the same intervals for food?

Coulson: Yes, just the same.

Third MP: Were the children excessively fatigued by this labor?

Coulson: Many times; we have cried often when we gave them the little food we had to give them. We had to shake them and they often fell asleep with the food in their mouths.

First MP: Had any of them any accident because of this labor?

Coulson: Yes, my eldest daughter when she went first there, while she was learning more about the work the foreman came by and said, "Ann, what are you doing there?" She said, "I am helping my friend." He said, "Let go, drop it this minute," and the cog caught her forefinger nail, and tore it off below the knuckle, and she was five weeks in Leeds Infirmary.

First MP: Has she lost that finger?

Coulson: It is cut off at the second joint.

Second MP: Were her wages paid during that time?

Coulson: No, sir, as soon as the accident happened, the wages were totally stopped. Indeed, I did not know how to get her cured, and I do not know how it could have been cured but for the Infirmary.

Second MP: Were the wages stopped at the half-day?

Coulson: She was stopped a quarter of a day; it was done about four o'clock.

First MP: Did the excessive term of labor occasion much cruelty also?

Coulson: Yes, with being so very much fatigued the strap was frequently used.

First MP: Have any of your children been whipped?

Coulson: Yes, every one. I was up in Lancashire a fortnight, and when I got home I saw my eldest daughter's shoulders and I said, "Ann, what's the matter?" She said, "The foreman has whipped me; but do not go to him for if you do we shall all lose our work." My wife was out at the time, and when she came in she said her back was beat nearly to a jelly.

Second MP: What were the wages in the regular hours?

Coulson: About seventy-five cents a week, each.

Second MP: When they worked those very long hours, how much did they get?

Coulson: About eighty-five cents.

Second MP: For all that additional labor they had only ten cents a week additional?

Coulson: No more.

First MP: Had your children any opportunity to rest during those long days of labor?

Coulson: No; whether there was work for them to do or not, they were told to keep moving backwards and forwards till something came to their hands.

First MP: At the time they worked those long hours, would it have been in their power to work a shorter number of hours?

Coulson: They must either go on at the long hours, or else be fired.

First MP: Thank you, Mr. Coulson. You've been very helpful.

(Coulson shuffles out, still twisting his cap and making a brief bow in the direction of his "betters.")

The purpose of the activity described in the classroom dialogue above was to help the student understand that the Industrial Revolution affected ordinary men, women, and children in many ways, not all of which were uniformly benign. By utilizing dramatization, the lessons to be learned were made vivid. By using source material, the students could appreciate that what they were dramatizing was not the invention of a fertile imagination alone. It was, instead, an original document, testimony actually offered to the members of Parliament in the very words of those who took part at the time. Source material may become musty with age and dusty from lack of use; nevertheless, within those documents, for those world history teachers who would search for them, lies an inexhaustible mine of material which curriculum bulletins and courses of study often filter out.

The frequent use of source materials in the world history classroom can do even more. It gives the students a chance to experience what the historian experiences when he or she works with sources in an effort to reconstruct the past. While our students of world history are not likely to become historians, it is not enough to tell them the facts. Nor is it enough to discuss in Socratic dialogue the implications of the facts in terms of the past, present, or future. Important as the facts are and as important as a discussion about those facts also is, students of world history should be given ample opportunity to examine historical documents so as to get a flavor of how the historian works as he or she pushes back the frontiers of knowledge in constant effort to ascertain what the facts really are.

Sources of Information in World History

Historians are not satisfied with the writings of others, but instead they insist upon using original sources of information. In parallel fashion, the world history teacher and the world history student should not be satisfied unless they, too, from time to time, examine original sources in their teaching and learning. Just as a river cannot rise above its source, so, too, one can go only so far in history by relying on the writings of others (i.e., secondary sources). Primary sources also must be used. "Because so much of history is remote and because the actors and witnesses have passed away, testimony is usually not oral, but written, and circumstantial evidence must be wrested from mute objects, the remains of former human activities."[1]

Historians and world history teachers may use records and remains, for both are useful in the teaching of world history. Records are documents which provide information. Usually they were written with specific purposes in mind. It is part of the task of the historian to ascertain what those purposes were or why the record was made. Not infrequently in history, the record was made to deceive both the present and the future historians, as much as to deceive everyone else. The teacher of world history who uses sources for instructional purposes should also try to ascertain why the document came to be made.

Among the records that a world history teacher may use are those that are both public and private. Among the former may be laws and records of the debates of lawmaking bodies, treaties and other diplomatic papers, court decisions and records of judicial proceedings, maps, charts, corporate documents, and documents of religious groups. Private records may include diaries, memoirs, letters, and wills. The songs, myths, ballads, and folk tales of a people are also useful records to examine.

In addition to studying records, the teacher of world history may examine with the class the remains of human life. Such remains may include the cooking and eating

[1] Allen Johnson, *The Historian and Historical Evidence*. New York: Charles Scribner's Sons, 1928, p. 3.

utensils a group used, a form of building in which the people once lived, a shrine at which they once worshiped, weapons with which they once fought enemies or went hunting, and a symbol they used in their religious worship. Weights and measures, coins and tools, roads and bridges, clothing, and cosmetics constitute some of the remains which an historian may use to reconstruct the past.

History has been called "the story of humankind." It is, but it is more than that. History is explanation in that the historian tries to describe not only what happened, but also to explain why it happened. History is in many ways both a science and an art. As a mode of inquiry, it has a method of investigation unique to it. However, more than most disciplines, it draws on the methods of inquiry used in other disciplines, as in geography, economics, sociology, anthropology, and, in more recent times, statistics. In addition to all of this, the historian approaches the tasks of reconstructing the past with a skeptical mind, one which questions even the most enduring commonly accepted beliefs. "Uncertainty about what is to be accepted as truth"[2] may be said to be the usual posture of the historian. This is not to say that everything is false and that truth is impossible. Nor is it to suggest that anything once disclosed need not be examined in the light of other truths. Nevertheless, in the words of Allen Johnson, "In historical studies doubt is the beginning of wisdom."[3]

The authenticity of historical documents is determined by subjecting the document to external and internal criticism. By external criticism, one means the process by which historians determine the document's authenticity. This they do by deciding who wrote the document, when it was written, and where it was written. Generally, a document the date of which cannot be determined is just about useless for historical purposes. Some features of a document may be more difficult to ascertain than may first appear. A document may contain a wrong date, either accidentally written or deliberately misdated. A document may say one thing, yet mean something else be-

cause of censorship. Also, a document may be written in one place, yet accurately describe circumstances in another. When, as during the so-called Glorious Revolution in England, censorship was rife, many authors had their books printed in Geneva or Holland. When censorship was enforced in France, critics of French society often wrote in England or Geneva.

The most important purpose of external criticism is to find out something about the author of the document being examined. Did the author know what he or she was writing about? How good was the writer as an observer? Was the author in a position to know? What were the author's religious beliefs? What was the author's social class and nationality? "The personal characteristics that make a writer a trustworthy witness or the reverse are of first importance."[4]

A document may also be subjected to internal criticism. The historian examines the source by verifying whether what is said in one part of the document is consistent with what is said in another. The data presented in the document must be supported by other evidence. In addition, the historian must have some understanding of the language used at the time the document was written; that is, the historian must know something of the literary style of the day, the idiomatic uses of language, and some of the colloquial expressions in common use.

In this chapter on the use of sources in the teaching of world history, a number of specific world history lessons making use of selected source materials are presented. It is suggested that these approaches to sources used by the historian form the basis of one or more lessons using a variety of records and remains. We do not propose a single mode of inquiry here. Instead, we suggest that the world history teacher and class examine these documents in a variety of ways, so as to reinforce growth in the knowledge, skills, and attitudes which are among the expected outcomes of world history instruction.

[2]G. Kitson Clark, *The Critical Historian*. New York: Basic Books, 1967, p. 97.

[3]Johnson, *op. cit.*, p. 50.

[4]*Ibid.*, p. 58.

Document #1:
A Letter to University Students

What follows is a letter written to a student at a university during the medieval period. At that time, getting an education was the privilege of the very few. Students in a medieval university had to suffer many hardships, including the lack of food and warmth. Then, as today, parents worried about the health of their children who were away at school. Read the excerpt below and discuss the questions which follow.

Beware of eating too much and too often, especially during the night. Avoid eating raw onions in the evening except rarely, because they dull the intellect and senses generally.

Avoid all very lacteal foods such as milk and fresh cheese except very rarely. Beware of eating milk and fish or milk and wine at the same meal, for milk and fish or milk and wine produce leprosy.

Don't have fresh pork too often. Salt pork is all right.

Don't eat many nuts except rarely and following fish. I say the same of meat and fruit, for they are bad and difficult to digest. . . .

Remember about the well water of Toulouse. Wherefore boil it, and the same with water of the Garonne, because such waters are bad.

Also, after you have risen from table, wash out your mouth with wine. . . .

Avoid sleeping on your back except rarely, for it has many disadvantages; but sleep on your side or stomach, and first on the right side, then on the left.

Don't sleep in winter with cold feet; but first warm them at the fire or by walking about or some other method. And in summer don't sleep with bed slippers on your feet, because they generate vapors which are very bad for the brain and memory. . . .

Likewise in winter keep your room closed from all noxious wind, and have straw on the pavement lest you suffer cold. . . .

Also, be well clad and well shod, and outdoors wear pattens,* to keep your feet warm. . . .

And when you see other students wearing their caps, . . . you do likewise, and if need be, put on one of fur. . . .

And when you go to bed at night, have a white nightcap on your head and beneath your cheeks, and another colored one over it, for at night the head should be kept warmer than during the day.

*pattens: overshoes.

Moreover, at the time of the great rains it is well to wear outdoors, over your cap, a bonnet or helmet of undressed skin; that is, a covering to keep the head from getting wet. . . .

Also, look after your stockings, and don't permit your feet to become dirty.

Also, wash the head, if you are accustomed to wash it, at least once a fortnight with hot lye and in a place sheltered from drafts, on the eve of a feast day toward nightfall. Then dry your hair with a brisk massage; afterward do it up; then put on a bonnet or cap.

Also, comb your hair daily if you will, morning and evening before eating or at least afterward, if you cannot do otherwise.

Also, look out that a draft does not strike you from window or crack while you study or sleep, or indeed at any time, for it strikes men without their noticing.

Also, in summer, in order not to have fleas or to have no more of them, sweep your room daily with a broom and not sprinkle it with water, for [fleas] are generated from damp dust. But you may spray it occasionally with strong vinegar, which comforts heart and brain.[5]

Questions for Students

1. When (approximately) do you think the letter was written? Why? By whom?

2. How is the medical advice offered here similar to or different from the good health habits encouraged today?

3. What does the letter reveal about university life in those days?

4. How might a historian use the document in writing an article on medieval education? On medieval health habits?

[5]Lynn Thorndike, *University Records and Life in the Middle Ages.* New York: Columbia University Press, 1944, pp. 156–159 *passim.* Used with permission.

Document #2:
Memories of Versailles

Louis XIV (1643–1715) was only five years old when he became king. By the time he began to rule in his own right in 1661, he already had a highly developed notion of absolutism and the divine right of kings, especially the divine place of Louis XIV. The court of Versailles was built to match the importance with which he viewed his place in history. What follows is a selection from the *Memoirs of the Duke of Saint Simon*.

At eight o'clock the chief *valet de chambre* on duty, who alone had slept in the royal chamber and who had dressed himself, awoke the King. The chief physician, the chief surgeon, and the nurse (as long as she lived) entered at the same time. The last kissed the King; the others rubbed and often changed his shirt, because he was in the habit of sweating a great deal. At the quarter, the grand chamberlain was called (or, in his absence, the first gentleman of the chamber), and those who had what was called the *grandes entrées*. The chamberlain (or chief gentleman) drew back the curtains, which had been closed again, and presented the holy water from the vase at the head of the bed. These gentlemen stayed but a moment, and that was the time to speak to the King if anyone had anything to ask of him, in which case the rest stood aside. When, contrary to custom, nobody had aught to say, they were there but for a few moments. He who had opened the curtains and presented the holy water presented also a prayerbook. Then all passed into the cabinet of the council. A very short religious service being over, the King called [and] they re-entered. The same officer gave him his dressing gown; immediately after, other privileged courtiers entered, and then everybody, in time to find the King putting on his shoes and stockings, for he did almost everything himself, and with address and grace. . . .

As soon as he was dressed, he prayed to God at the side of his bed, where all the clergy present knelt, the cardinals without cushions, all the laity remaining standing; and the captain of the guards came to the balustrade during the prayer, after which the King passed into his cabinet.

He found there, or was followed by all who had the *entrée*, a very numerous company, for it included everybody in any office. He gave orders to each for the day; thus within a half [or] a quarter of an hour it was known what he meant to do; and then all this crowd left direct-ly. . . . It was then a good opportunity for talking with the King, for example, about plans of gardens and buildings. . . .

The King gave audiences when he wished to accord any, spoke with whomever he might wish to speak secretly to, and gave secret interviews to foreign ministers. . . .

The King went to Mass, where his musicians always sang an anthem. While he was going to and returning from Mass, everybody spoke to him who wished, after apprising the captain of the guard if they were not distinguished. The King, upon returning from Mass, asked almost immediately for the council. Then the morning was finished.

On Sunday, and often on Monday, there was a council of state; on Tuesday a finance council; on Wednesday council of state; on Saturday finance council. Rarely were two held in one day or any on Thursday or Friday. . . .

Thursday morning was almost always blank. It was the day for audiences that the King wished to give—often unknown to any—backstair audiences. . . .

The dinner was always *au petit couvert*; that is, the King ate by himself in his chamber, upon a square table in front of the middle window. It was more or less abundant, for he ordered in the morning whether it was to be "a little" or "very little" service. But even at this last, there were always many dishes and three courses without counting the fruit. . . .

Grand dinners were very rare and only took place on grand occasions, and then ladies were present. . . .

The King was fond of air, and when deprived of it his health suffered; he had headaches . . . caused by the undue use he had formerly made of perfumes, so that for many years he could not endure any except the odor of orange flowers; therefore if you had to approach anywhere near him you did well not to carry them.

As he was but little sensitive to heat or cold or even to rain, the weather was seldom sufficiently bad to prevent his going abroad. He went out for three objects: stag hunting, once or more each week; shooting in his parks (and no man handled a gun with more grace or skill), once or twice each week; and walking in his gardens for exercise and to see his workmen. . . .

At ten o'clock his supper was served. . . . This supper was always on a grand scale, the royal household (that is, the sons and daughters of France) at table, and a large number of courtiers and ladies present, sitting or standing.

After supper the King stood some moments, his back to the balustrade of the foot of his bed, encircled by all his Court; then, with bows to the ladies, passed into his cabinet, where on arriving he gave his orders. He passed a little less than an hour there, seated in an armchair, with his children and his grandchildren, and their husbands or wives.

The King, wishing to retire, went and fed his dogs; then said good night, passed into his chamber, . . . where he said his prayers as in the morning, then undressed. He said good night with an inclination of the head, and while everybody was leaving the room stood at the corner of the mantelpiece, where he gave the order to the colonel of the guards alone. Then commenced what was called the *petit coucher*, at which only the specially privileged remained. That was short. They did not leave until he got into bed. It was a moment to speak to him. Then all left.[6]

Questions for Students

1. Why are memoirs suspect as historical sources?

2. In view of these suspicions, what cautions must an historian exercise in using memoirs in trying to explain the past?

3. Why is it important to know how long after the events described took place that they were written down?

4. What would you need to know about the writer in order to evaluate the accuracy of what he wrote?

5. Frame an hypothesis about life at the court of Versailles at the height of the powers of Louis XIV. How would you test your hypothesis?

---

[6]*Memoirs of the Duke of Saint-Simon on the Reign of Louis XIV and the Regency*. Translated by Bayle St. John. London: Bickers and Sons, 1880, Volume III, pp. 21–27 *passim*.

Document #3:
The London Fire of 1666

The selection below contains an account of the great fire of London in 1666, just a year after the great bubonic plague struck England. Many of the English were convinced that the plague and fire were brought about by the immorality at the court of Charles II.

The Fire, 1666

September 2. This fatal night about ten began the deplorable fire, near Fish Street, in London.

September 3. The fire having continued all this night (if I may call that night which was light as day for ten miles about, after a dreadful manner), when conspiring with a fierce eastern wind in a very dry season, I went on foot to the same place; and saw the whole south part of the city burning from Cheapside to the Thames, and all along Cornhill (for it likewise kindled back against the wind as well as forward). . . . The conflagration was so universal and the people so astonished that from the beginning, I know not by what despondency or fate, they hardly stirred to quench it; so that there was nothing heard or seen but crying out and lamentation, running about like distracted creatures, without at all attempting to save even their goods; such a strange consternation there was upon them, so [that] it burned both in breadth and length the churches, public halls, Exchange, hospitals, monuments, and ornaments; leaping after a prodigious manner from house to house and street to street, at great distances one from the other. For the heat, with a long set of fair and warm weather, had even ignited the air and prepared the materials to conceive the fire, which devoured, after an incredible manner, houses, furniture, and everything. Here we saw the Thames covered with goods floating, all the barges and boats laden with what some had time and courage to save, as on the other side the carts, etc., carrying out to the fields, which for many miles were strewn with movables of all sorts, and erecting tents to shelter both people and what goods they could get away. Oh, the miserable and calamitous spectacle, such as haply the world had not seen since the foundation of it, nor can be outdone till the universal conflagration thereof. All the sky was of a fiery aspect, like the top of a burning oven, and the light seen above forty miles round about for many nights. God grant mine eyes may never behold the like, who now saw above 10,000 houses all in one flame! The noise and cracking and thunder of the impetuous flames, the shrieking of women and children, the hurry of people, the fall of towers, houses, and churches was like a hideous storm; and the air all about so hot and inflamed that at the least one was not able to approach it, so that they were forced to stand still and let

Document #4:
No Strangers Need Apply

In 1854 Commodore Perry with a fleet of American ships forced the Japanese to open their ports to world trade. The modernization and westernization of Japan may be said to date from that time. What is less well known is that in 1636 the government of Japan tightly shut Japan off from any foreign contact. What follows is a statement from the Act of Seclusion of 1636.

1. Japanese ships shall by no means be sent abroad.

2. No Japanese shall be sent abroad. Anyone violating this prohibition shall suffer the penalty of death, and the shipowner and crew shall be held up together with the ship.

3. All Japanese residing abroad shall be put to death when they return home.

4. All Christians shall be examined by official examiners.

5. Informers against Christians shall be rewarded.

6. The arrival of foreign ships must be reported . . . and watch kept over them.

7. The Namban people (Spaniards or Portuguese) and any other people with evil titles propagating Christianity shall be incarcerated in the Omura prison as before.

8. Even ships shall not be left untouched in the matter of exterminating Christians.

9. Everything shall be done in order to see

the flames burn on, which they did, for near two miles in length and one in breadth. The clouds also of smoke were dismal, and reached, upon computation, near fifty miles in length. . . . London was, but is no more! . . .

September 5. It now pleased God, by abating the wind, and by the industry of the people, when almost all was lost, infusing a new spirit into them, that the fury began to abate about noon, so as it came no farther than the Temple westward nor than the entrance of Smithfield north: but continued all this day and night so impetuous toward Cripplegate and the Tower as made us all despair. It also broke out again in the Temple, but the courage of the multitude persisting, and many houses being blown up, such gaps and desolations were soon made, as with the former three days' consumption, the back fire did not so vehemently urge upon the rest as formerly. There was yet no standing near the burning and glowing ruins by near a furlong's space. . . .

September 7. I went this morning on foot, . . . with extraordinary difficulty, clambering over heaps of yet smoking rubbish, and frequently mistaking where I was; the ground under my feet so hot that it even burnt the soles of my shoes. . . .

The people who now walked about the ruins appeared like men in some dismal desert, or rather, in some great city laid waste by a cruel enemy; to which was added the stench that came from some poor creatures' bodies, beds, and other combustible goods. . . .

I then went toward Islington and Highgate, where one might have seen 200,000 people of all ranks and degrees dispersed, and lying along by their heaps of what they could save from the fire, deploring their loss; and though ready to perish for hunger and destitution, yet not asking one penny for relief, which to me appeared a stranger sight than any I had yet beheld. His Majesty and Council indeed took all imaginable care for their relief by proclamation for the country to come in and refresh them with provisions.[7]

Questions for Students

1. Distinguish between a diary and a memoir as an historical source.

2. What precautions must the historian take in using diaries as historical sources?

3. What must historians know about the writer in evaluating the description of the London fire?

4. How would you test the accuracy of what the observer noted?

5. Fires are always dangerous. Why was this particularly so during the seventeenth century?

[7]*The Fire, 1666*, from *The Diary of John Evelyn*, edited by William Bray. Akron, Ohio: St. Dunstan Society, 1901, Volume II, pp. 20–25.

---

that no Christian is survived by descendants, and anyone disregarding this injunction shall be put to death, while proper punishment shall be meted out to the other members of his family according to their deeds.

10. Children born of the Namban people (Spaniards or Portuguese) in Nagasaki and people adopting these Namban children into their family shall be put to death; capital punishment shall also be meted out to those Namban descendants if they return to Japan, and their relatives in Japan, who may communicate with them, shall receive sutiable punishment.

11. The samurai [warrior aristocracy of Japan] shall not purchase goods on board foreign ships directly from foreigners.[8]

[8]Y. Takekoshi, *The Economic Aspects of the History of the Civilization of Japan*. London: George Allen & Unwin, Ltd., 1930, Volume II, p. 129. Used with permission.

Questions for Students

1. What was the attitude of the Japanese government of 1636 toward Spanish, Portuguese, and Christians generally?

2. Frame an hypothesis with regard to Japan's attitude toward foreigners at this time.

3. Does the document itself help you to frame an hypothesis? How?

4. How would you test your hypothesis?

Document #5:
Preparing to Enter Government Service in the China of Old

Civil service examinations were used in China by the middle of the second century B.C. What is described here is the examination a distinguished scholar took during the twelfth century. Without passing the examinations a career in military or government service was closed.

Read the selection below and answer the questions which follow:

> The time for the palace examinations came. Ouyang Shiu was nominated by the Emperor to be chief examiner, together with a number of distinguished scholars as judges. The approach to this most critical moment of a scholar's life was always filled with keen excitement, tense hope, and a nervous fear of failure. It was the moment to which all his years of grinding labor and hours of burning the midnight oil were supposed to lead. The candidates had to get up in the middle of the night and come to the palace at dawn, bringing their cold meals with them, for they would not be able to leave until the examinations were over. During the examinations they were shut up in cubicles under the supervision of palace guards. There was a rigorous system to prevent bribery or favoritism. The candidates' papers were recopied by official clerks before they were submitted to the examiners, to avoid recognition of their identity by their handwriting. In the recopied papers the writers' names were taken out and kept on file. While the candidates were left out after the examinations, the judges themselves were shut up within the palace and forbidden to have any contact with the people outside, usually from late January till early March, until the papers were properly graded and submitted to the Emperor. The candidates were examined first on questions of history or principles of government. There was a second examination on the classics, and finally, after the successful ones had been graded, there was one—under the direct supervision of the Emperor—on lyrics, descriptive poetry, and again, essays on politics. Emperor Jentsung was especially anxious to recruit good talent for his government and took a personal interest in these tests. He sent out the subjects for the papers by his own personal servants and sometimes, to avoid leakage, changed them at the last moment. . . .[9]

Questions for Students

1. What is the purpose of a civil service examination today? To what extent is the purpose similar to or different from that of ancient China?

2. How do you explain why mastery of the Confucian classics was required, rather than demonstrated accomplishment in the skills needed for government service?

3. Was great importance attached to the examinations? How can you tell?

4. What advantages and disadvantages are there in such emphasis on examinations as a basis of judging merit for government service? What alternatives would you propose? Why would you propose them?

5. Do you suppose there was much cheating in the examinations? How would an historian find out?

[9]Lin Yutang, *The Gay Genius: The Biography of Su Tungpo*. New York: The John Day Company, Inc., 1947, pp. 38–40 *passim*. Used with permission.

Document #6:
Mexico City in Montezuma's Time

This document may be distributed to the students without identifying it. Based on internal evidence ask the students the following:

1. Identify the place being described.
2. Identify the writer who is describing it.
3. Determine the approximate time when the description might have been written.
4. How able an observer is the writer? How can you tell?

This city has many public squares in which are situated the markets and other places for buying and selling. There is one square twice as large as that of the city of Salamanca, surrounded by porticos where are daily assembled more than sixty thousand souls, engaged in buying and selling, and where are found all kinds of merchandise that the world affords, embracing the necessaries of life, as for instance articles of food, as well as jewels of gold and silver, lead, brass, copper, tin, precious stones, bone shells, snails, and feathers. There are also exposed for sale wrought and unwrought stone, bricks burnt and unburnt, timber hewn and unhewn, of different sorts.

There is a street for game, where every variety of birds found in the country are sold, as fowls, partridges, quails, wild ducks, fly-catchers, widgeons, turtledoves, pigeons, reedbirds, parrots, sparrows, eagles, hawks, owls, and kestrels; they sell likewise the skins of some birds of prey, with their feathers, head, beak and claws. There are also sold rabbits, hares, deer, and little dogs, which are raised for eating. There is also an herb street, where may be obtained all sorts of roots and medicinal herbs that the country affords. There are apothecaries' shops, where prepared medicines, liquids, ointments, and plasters are sold; barbers' shops, where they wash and shave the head; and restauranteurs, that furnish food and drink at a certain price.

There is also a class of men like those called in Castile porters, for carrying burthens. Woods and coals are seen in abundance, and braziers of earthenware for burning coals; mats of various kinds for beds, others of a lighter sort for seats, and for halls and bedrooms. There are all kinds of green vegetables, especially onions, leeks, garlic, watercress, nasturium, borage, sorrel, artichokes, and golden thistle; fruits also of numerous descriptions, amongst which are cherries and plums, similar to those in Spain.

Every kind of merchandise is sold in a particular street or quarter assigned to it exclusively, and thus the best order is preserved. They sell everything by number or measure; at least so far we have not observed them to sell anything by weight. There is a building in the great square that is used as an audience house, where ten or twelve persons, who are magistrates, sit and decide all controversies that arise in the market, and order delinquents to be punished. In the same square there are other persons who go constantly about among the people observing what is sold, and the measures used in selling; and they have been seen to break measures that were not true.[10]

---

[10]From Hernando Cortez, *Despatches to Emperor Charles V.* New York: 1843, pp. 112–114.

Document #7:
The Trial of King Charles I

The document below, with all identification removed, may be presented to students. Students should be able to answer the following questions:

1. What appears to be taking place?
2. Who is being punished, and who is doing the punishing? How can you tell?
3. To whom does the author seem sympathetic? How can you tell?
4. What appears to be the attitude of the king towards "divine right"?
5. What would you want to know about the observer when evaluating the document in an historical study?

When he was first brought to Westminster Hall, which was upon the twentieth of January, 1649, before the high court of justice, he looked upon them and sat down without any manifestation of trouble, never doffing his hat. . . . He was impeached for . . . treasons and crimes . . . as a tyrant, traitor, and murderer, and a public enemy to the commonwealth of England. . . . President Bradshaw, after he had insolently reprimanded the king for not having doffed his hat or showing more respect . . . asked the king what answer he made to that impeachment.

The king . . . told them he would first know of them by what authority they presumed by force to bring him before them, and who gave them power to judge his actions, for which he was accountable to none but to God. . . . He told them that he was their king and they his subjects, who owed him duty and obedience; that no parliament had authority to call him before them. . . . As there were many persons present at that woeful spectacle who felt a real compassion for the king, so there were others of so barbarous and brutal a behavior toward him that they called him . . . murderer; and one spat in his face which His Majesty without expressing any resentment wiped off with his handkerchief. . . .

Of the execution of the sentence . . . no more shall be said here of that lamentable tragedy, so much to the dishonor of the nation . . .[11]

---

[11]From *The History of the Rebellion*, by Edward Hyde, first Earl of Clarendon (1609–1674), found in *Readings in Medieval and Modern History*, edited by Hutton Webster. Boston: D. C. Heath and Company, 1971.

Document #8:
The Defeat of the King of the Matabele

The African kings and tribal chiefs, helpless against the white man and his guns, nevertheless fought for survival. Lo Bengula, King of the Matabele, after skillful negotiation, was finally forced to submit. To Cecil Rhodes he gave vast lands and rich mining rights.

It was the critical moment. For a while no one spoke. The proposed Concession lay on the table. The massive bronze figure of Lo Bengula loomed large in the eyes of those standing around, and his inscrutable and bloodshot eyes sent a thrill through the assembly. Then, after an ominous pause, the King lurched suddenly forward, seized a pen, and affixed his mark. Had he been able to forecast the future, a massacre and not a treaty would have received his sanction. But the recent visit of Sir Sidney Shippard, who was accompanied by Colonel Goold-Adams and the Bishop of Bloemfontein, . . . had apparently convinced him that his true interest lay in conciliating the English rather than the Boer element in his territory. . . . Here is the . . . text of the grant:

Know all men by these presents, that whereas Charles Dunell Rudd, of Kimberley; Rochfort Maguire, of London; and Francis Robert Thompson, of Kimberley, hereinafter called the grantees, have . . . agreed . . . to pay to me, my heirs, and successors the sum of one hundred pounds sterling, British currency, on the first day of every lunar month; and, further, to deliver at my royal kraal [village] one thousand Martini-Henry breech-loading rifles, together with one hundred thousand rounds of suitable ball cartridge; . . . and further, to deliver on the Zambezi River a steamboat with guns suitable for defensive purposes upon the said river, or in lieu of the said steamboat, should I so elect, to pay me the sum of five hundred pounds sterling, British currency. On the execution of these presents, I, Lo Bengula, King of Matabeleland, Mashonaland, and other adjoining territories, in exercise of my sovereign powers, . . . do hereby grant . . . unto the said grantees . . . the complete and exclusive charge over all metals and minerals situated and contained in my kingdoms, principalities, and dominions, together with full power to do all things that they may deem necessary to win and procure the same, and to hold, collect, and enjoy the profits and revenues, if any, derivable from the said metals and minerals, subject to the aforesaid payment; and whereas I have been much molested of late by divers persons seeking and desiring to obtain grants and concessions of land and mining rights in my territories, I do hereby authorize the said grantees . . . to take all necessary and lawful steps to exclude from my kingdom, principalities, and dominions all persons seeking land, metals, minerals, or mining rights therein, and I do hereby undertake to render them all such needful assistance as they may from time to time require for the exclusion of such persons, and to grant no concessions of land or mining rights from and after this date without their consent and concurrence. . . .

This, given under my hand this thirtieth day of October, in the year of our Lord 1888, at my royal kraal.　　　　LO BENGULA X HIS MARK
　　　　　　　　　　　　C. D. RUDD
　　　　　　　　　　　　ROCHFORT MAGUIRE
　　　　　　　　　　　　F. R. THOMPSON[12]

[12]Lewis Mitchell, *The Life and Times of the Rt. Hon. Cecil John Rhodes*. London: Edward Arnold, Ltd., 1912, Volume I, pp. 255–257.

Questions for Students

1. What would you want to know about the writer in order to determine how reliable an eyewitness account this is?
2. What does the account reveal about the role of the whites? Select those portions of the account that justify your answer.
3. What does it reveal about the role of the blacks? Select those portions of the account that justify your answer.
4. How does the eyewitness know that had the king "been able to forecast the future, a massacre and not a treaty would have received his sanction"?
5. How does the eyewitness know that the king was convinced that a treaty was the best step he could take?

Document #9:
The Fourteen Points
and the Atlantic Charter

Summaries of the Fourteen Points and the Atlantic Charter may be distributed to students without identification. From reading the documents, the students should be asked:

1. Identify each.
2. When was each written?
3. By whom?
4. What similarities may be found between them?
5. What differences may be found between them?
6. What do they reveal about the circumstances under which they came to be written?

SUMMARIES

There should be no secret treaties.

There should be freedom of the seas for all.

Trade between nations should flow more freely.

Armaments should be reduced.

The rights of the peoples not living in their own lands should be respected.

Foreign troops should be taken out of places where they are not wanted.

A League of Nations should be formed whose job it would be to keep peace among nations.

There should be no territorial changes that do not agree with the wishes of the people.

All people should choose the form of government they wish.

All nations should enjoy the world's trade and raw materials equally.

All nations would work together to improve labor standards, economic advancement, and social security.

There should be a peace which would allow people to live in freedom from fear and want.

All nations should be able to cross the seas without interference.

The use of force would be abandoned.

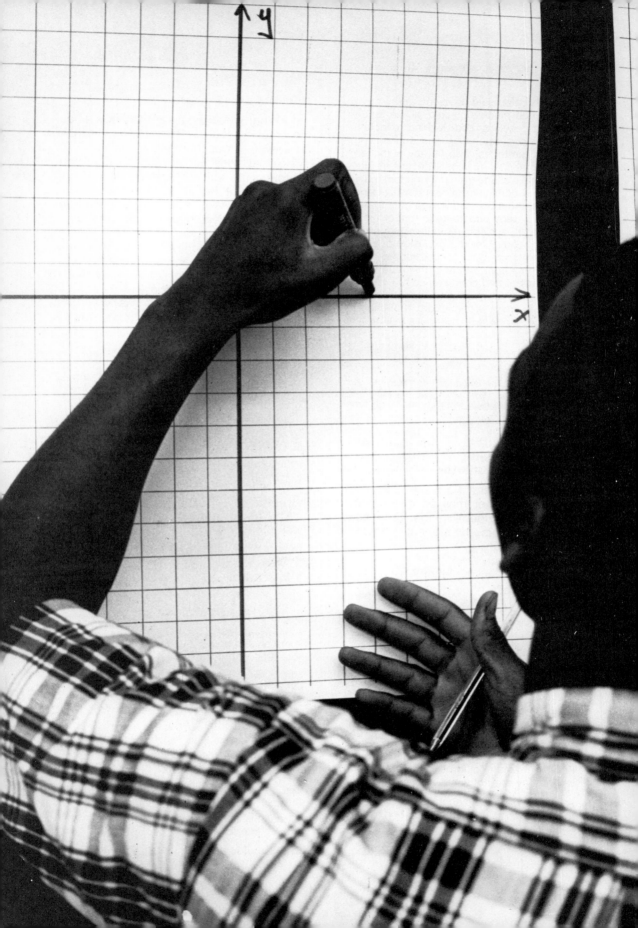

6

World History: Skills Development

Ms. Berra's ninth year class is in the early stages of a three-week unit on the study of Africa. Specifically, the aim of the unit is "Why is Africa a continent in revolution?" The pupils have divided themselves into committees, each committee taking one of the newer African nations. Committee work has not yet begun because Ms. Berra is determined that before research activities are undertaken, the class should have a sound grasp of the geography of the continent of Africa as a whole. Two class lessons are set aside, each to be devoted to the physical characteristics of African geography. There is a large roll-down map of Africa, and each student has a textbook and a simple outline map of Africa as well.

Ms. Berra: Africa's physical geography has sometimes been compared to that of an inverted saucer. (*She draws the diagram on the board.*) Why?

Susan: Africa is an inverted saucer because it has narrow coastal plains and most of it is made up of plateaus.

Ms. Berra: Would you go to the map in front of the room and, using the color key, see if what Susan said is correct? Angelo?

Angelo: I don't see any key.

Ms. Berra: Would you help him, Bill?

Bill: I don't see any key either.

Ms. Berra: Perhaps Margaret can help us?

Margaret (*walks slowly to the board*): I think the key you mean is the color key in this box. The dark green is for areas of rain forest, the light green for lowlands, and the dark brown is for high peaks.

Ms. Berra: Now, using the key as Margaret described it, would you go to the map and see if

Susan is right? Angelo?

Angelo (*saunters to the map*): Well, the coast is kind of light in color so it is a lowland. Most of the rest of Africa seems higher because of the brownish color.

Thomas (*calling out from his seat*): Yeah, most of Africa is made up of plateaus and grasslands.

Ms. Berra: You're right, but your contribution would have been more valuable if you hadn't called out. Could you find areas that are exceptions to the plateau and grassland features of Africa? Bill?

Bill (*walks to the map*): Part of the area here seems to be dark green in color and must be rain forest. (*He waves his finger in the general direction of the coloring.*)

Ms. Berra: Could you be more specific, Bill?

Bill: Right here in Africa.

Ms. Berra: Would you identify the areas Bill is pointing to more specifically, Margo?

Margo: The dark green means that the area is tropical rain forest in climate, and I think that the area Bill pointed to was the Congo and part of Nigeria too.

Ms. Berra: You're right and that's very good. Now let's see if each of you can make a map of Africa in which you show the main features of Africa's topography and climate. With a similar color scheme, take the outline maps you have, and using the map in your text and the wall map, prepare your own map of Africa. I'll help you until the bell rings, so do as much of it as you can. Take the outline map home and finish the job for homework. (*The class gets to work, and Ms. Berra walks about the room giving individual help to as many pupils as time permits.*)

Locating and Gathering Information

A balanced world history program should give students opportunities at appropriate points throughout their school years to locate and use effectively a variety of instructional resources, including reading materials, audio-visual presentations, and community resources. Such materials are the sources for research and information-gathering activities in world history programs. Class discussion, panels, essays, research papers, reports, and the preparation of graphic materials depend on the effective use of all these instructional resources.[1]

The principal source of information usually available to the secondary school pupil is the textbook. Instruction in use of the textbook as a source of information should come on two occasions: first, when the textbooks are distributed at the start of the school year; second, when specific world history assignments require the use of the textbook.

The first, or extrinsic, approach capitalizes on the natural interest aroused in the students with the receipt of a new or different textbook. The second, or intrinsic, kind of lesson, concerned with a specific assignment involving the textbook, comes after the initial training lessons in the use of the textbook. This may take the form of open book or supervised study lessons.

Time is given in class for the students to do an assignment which involves the seeking of information about a particular topic in the textbook. This should involve use of the index and the table of contents, interpretations of reading matter, understanding of a chart or graph, noting an illustration, etc. As the class works at the assignment, the teacher circulates about the room, helping here, encouraging there, always available to answer questions and to guide. Where a series of such lessons are contemplated, though it is not necessarily on successive days, it would be wise to have on hand in the classroom a full set of textbooks for use by the students. This relieves them of carrying the book to and from school—helpful in view of the size and weight of the newer textbooks—and relieves the teacher of penalizing those who forgot their textbooks.

The library, of course, is another major source of information. Instruction in world history should also include instruction in the use of the library and should provide opportunities for the application of the library skills. Here again, instruction can be both extrinsic and intrinsic—that is, there can be lessons in the library in which the subject is the library resources, and there can be lessons involving subject matter and how the resources of the library can be used to acquire information about the subject. In the former, the library lesson, it is wise to enlist the assistance of the school librarian. In some communities, where the librarian is licensed as a teacher of library or librarian-

[1]See Ella C. Leppert, "Locating and Gathering Information," in *Skill Development in Social Studies*, edited by Helen McCracken Carpenter, 33rd Yearbook. Washington, D.C.: National Council for the Social Studies, 1963, p. 53.

teacher, it is expected that the librarian be used for such instruction.

Instruction must be provided in the use of newspapers, one the most important sources of information about current happenings. As with the textbook, instruction must be provided students in the makeup of the standard newspaper: the news section (frequently divided into international, national, state, and local news), financial section, sports pages, society pages, obituary columns, entertainment section, book reviews, editorial columns, and special features (cartoons, letters, etc.). The significant differences between the news pages and the editorial columns should be made clear to the class. The study of the newspaper provides an excellent opportunity to invite the local editor to speak to the class and/or have the class visit the local newspaper offices and plant.

Evaluating Information

Subjected to a bombardment of facts and of opinions masquerading as facts, it is a wise adult who can think his or her way through to an honest opinion. What to believe and what not to believe are basic problems in selecting, organizing, and evaluating information. It is not just a question of sorting the true from the untrue but of recognizing half-truths, exaggerations, misstatements of facts, opinions represented as facts, and hasty generalizations. Students need an educational program in which they are made aware of the problem and in which they can develop the techniques and

habits of thinking to cope with the problem.

In their reading and discussion, students should be led to recognize the value of authorities read, quoted, cited, heard, or otherwise noted. They must be able to determine what people and publications are authoritative, what organizations can be relied upon to gather and present facts honestly, and what are the special interests and blind spots of people, publications, and organizations.

Students should be taught to recognize the following false authorities:

1. **The authority of tradition.** "What was good enough for my grandfather and for my father is good enough for me." "We've always done it that way." The past, it must be noted, is not the present; the times of grandfather are not the times of today. Today's problems demand other means and methods.

2. **"Get-on-the-bandwagon" authority.** This technique operates on the assumption that the majority is always right and that it is best to be part of that majority. It includes the appeal to numbers. "Everybody says that machines are displacing people at a faster and faster rate. Automation is at the root of our troubles. Everyone says so." "Thousands flocked to the side of Napoleon after his escape from Elba. France wanted him back." Demand proof when the words "everyone" and "thousands" are used. Think it through.

3. **Testimonial authority.** Here we go from the majority to the individual. The most

common application of this authority is in advertisements using stars of the sports or entertainment worlds to endorse a certain brand of cigarettes or a beauty preparation. "If it's good enough for them, it is good enough for you." An extension of this authority is the public figure in one field who offers advice and views in fields in which he or she has little competence; for example, the admiral who gives advice on an educational system or the auto manufacturer who suggests improvements in a welfare system.

4. **The authority of the printed word.** It is a common practice to use a newspaper or periodical article as an authority to support a point of view. By comparing the treatment of the same news event in two or three papers, students will realize that news reporting is often slanted. They can then conclude that newspapers and magazines often reflect the particular points of view of the owners and management. While it is comparatively easy for students to recognize the different points of view in comparing *The Worker* with *The Chicago Tribune*, it is less easy for them to see the different editorial policies of *The New York Times* and *The World Journal Tribune* or *The St. Louis Post-Dispatch* and *The Philadelphia Inquirer*. Periodicals also differ in the kinds of articles printed and in the presentation of information. The *New Republic* should be compared with the *National Review*, and *Time* should be compared with *Newsweek*.

Facts must be differentiated from opinions and assumptions. We must provide our students with the tools and skills by which they can recognize faulty reasoning when they see it or hear it. The following are some of the fallacies of reasoning, logic, and reporting found in many of our news and information media. Students should be trained to recognize each of them.

● **The irrelevancy of statements.** "Ed Jones would make a fine administrator. After all, he belongs to the country club." The second part of the statement has nothing to do with Jones's competency as an administrator.

● **The assumption of conclusions.** "All students at State University are disloyal. After all, if they weren't disloyal they wouldn't go to State University." The second statement or conclusion is only a rewording of the first sentence or premise and contains no additional information.

● **The use of platitudes.** A platitude is a generalization that has been said so many times over so long a period that an unthinking individual may accept it as truth. "Woman's place is in the home." "You can't change human nature."

● **The illogic of if-then.** "If the government would cut out the nonsense of spending so much trying to get to the moon, then we would have better schools, hospitals, and recreational facilities." The "then" part does not necessarily follow from the "if" part; too many steps in the process between the "if" and the "then" are skipped.

● **The false analogy.** "Jim's father was a high school dropout. What can we expect of Jim?" The reasons for the father's leaving school do not necessarily apply to Jim.

● **The changing of definitions.** "A good superintendent of schools should have experience on all levels, be a good administrator, and develop policy. Edwards would make a good superintendent because he has a State certificate and many influential friends." Notice how the definition of a good superintendent has shifted.

● **The use of ridicule.** Ridicule to denigrate a point of view is frequently used. "The *so-called* policy of détente of our *head-in-the-clouds* liberal President is an example of the *pie-in-the-sky* world politics being played." Notice the ridicule of the italicized words.

In a similar way, students should receive instruction in the nature of propaganda; and, given the tools and skills, should be able to recognize and combat propaganda. Among the propagandist's techniques are the following:

● **Name calling.** This technique tries to make people form judgments by attaching a bad name to individuals, groups, nations, races, beliefs, and so on. For example, French—Frogs, bankers—economic royalists, union leaders—pinkos, intellectuals—eggheads.

● **Glittering generalities.** This technique attaches "good" names to persons and policies so that we may accept them without really looking into the evidence. Thus, if the British are accepted as "freedom loving," how can their programs be questioned? The possibility of arguing with a proposal endorsed by the Chamber of Commerce is decreased if the generalization is accepted that business people are the "industrial brains" of the nation.

• **Transfer.** The writer or speaker attempts to attach the authority and prestige of something we respect to the thing he or she hopes we will accept or reject. Price-fixing laws protect "free enterprise." Or, on the other hand, the propagandist seeks to have his or her readers or listeners react negatively to a matter he or she wants them to reject. Social security is "creeping socialism." Truth in labeling is "government interference."

• **Plain folks.** It is used to win our confidence by pointing out that a leading figure or a prominent politician is just like the rest of us. Used particularly around election time.

• **Card stacking.** Rather than indicate the truths and benefits on both sides of an argument, the propagandist will completely ignore those aspects with which he or she is not in sympathy and hammer away at the so-called evils and disadvantages.

Developing Map and Globe Skills

By the time the student reaches the junior high school, almost every subskill associated with interpreting maps and globes has been introduced, and the task of the junior high school teacher is to develop these skills systematically. By the time the student reaches the senior high school, all subskills should have been introduced through planned experiences and systematic development. The task of the senior high school world history teacher is thus to reteach, maintain, and extend these skills.

In the sequential development of special understandings, the study of a globe precedes the study of a map. Whereas a map is not an accurate representation of the earth's surface, a globe does represent more truly the surface of the earth in shapes, distances, directions, and relative sizes. The study of the globe is essential to an understanding of the position of the earth

in its relationship to the solar system. Maps and globes develop a sense of place and space so very important in the study of geography, economics, and history.

Many abilities are involved in the development of skills in map and globe interpretation. There may be said to be six basic groupings for a program of instruction:

1. Ability to orient the map and to note directions.
2. Ability to recognize the scale of a map and to compute distances.
3. Ability to locate places on maps and globes by means of grid systems.
4. Ability to express relative locations.
5. Ability to read map symbols.
6. Ability to compare maps and to make inferences.[2]

The importance of each of these abilities should be clear. The ability to orient maps involves the knowledge of directions. Students should be able to orient themselves with respect to directions to their homes and school, the classroom, and the school cafeteria. In the absence of specific indication, pupils should know that "up" is not always north and "down" not always south. The ability to compute distances involves the ability to recognize and use the scale of a map. The whole concept of scale and distance involves the relation of the map to reality. Comparing may be with ground distances familiar to the student; comparing distances by auto routes and "as the crow flies" are applicable activities. An understanding of grid systems, whether latitude or longitude of the usual map or the alphabetical-numerical grid of the road map, is essential to the student's ability to locate places. The ability to express relative locations involves the ability to see the total picture presented by the map. The student must become aware that topographical features—mountains, rivers, deserts—may make actual "human" distances quite different from geographical distances. Such an awareness requires an increased degree of sophistication on the part of the pupil. The ability to read symbols makes the

[2]Clyde F. Kohn, "Interpreting Maps and Globes," *Skills in Social Studies*, edited by Helen McCracken Carpenter. 24th Yearbook. Washington, D.C.: National Council for the Social Studies, 1953, pp. 146–147.

map come alive, for these keys to the language of maps represent geographic and cultural phenomena. Finally, the ability to compare maps and to make inferences is the crowning skill requiring the highest level of awareness and understanding. This ability represents the drawing together of the other five abilities and can make the use of maps in the world history classroom an integral part of the learning process instead of a mere adjunct.

Generally speaking, for the world history teacher the program of instruction in map skills involves a systematic consolidation and extension, rather than an introduction which takes place in the primary and intermediate grades.

Understanding Time and Chronology

As teachers of world history, we are so concerned with covering great sweeps of time or with concentrating on relatively narrow stretches of years that in either case we tend to neglect developing in our students the concepts of time and chronology. We move so rapidly through courses in world history, covering more than 6,000 years of history in a school year, that the edges of the chronological frame of reference are at the best blurred, and, at the worse, nonexistent. The panoramas, images, and personalities fly about so fast that within a relatively short period the time relationships lose all meaning.

This is not to say that we should return to the older method of history as a study of dates. When students ask "Do we have to know dates?", we must be extremely careful in what we answer. We do not insist that pupils memorize lists of dates and events so as to be able to recite them from memory, but we do want them to know dates and events in relation to other dates and events. In short, students should understand cause and effect in the chronological sense. Today it is thought that an understanding of time and chronology is more clearly revealed through a person's ability to perceive relationships among events than through his memorizing lists of unconnected events.

To develop time and chronology skills in the secondary school, attention must be focused on the following: (1) understanding the measurement and vocabulary of time;

(2) understanding past cultures as the bases for the traditions and customs of the present; and (3) understanding change and continuity against the background of time. Instruction in these basic understandings cannot be restricted to one aspect at a time, but rather must be developed simultaneously with the skills in many areas.

Students should know how historical time is measured. How many students know how to count the number of years, say, between 1320 B.C. and 476 A.D.? How many understand the concept of B.C. and A.D.? How many are aware of the differences in the various calendars: Julian and Gregorian, lunar and solar, Hebraic and Islamic?

Instruction must be provided on a systematic basis in the use and understanding of the vocabulary of time. Students are familiar with definite terms, such as year, century, decade, and mid-century. Understanding of less definite terms, such as ancient times, medieval period, the modern era, and the period of the Renaissance, is no less important. The many indefinite terms— "in colonial days," "many years ago," "in the near future," "in the days of our forefathers," "several centuries ago"—must be made more definite whenever possible.

The world history teacher must take every possible opportunity to review these words and concepts as instruction proceeds. Frequent reference to a large wall-sized time line running across the front of the room above the board helps to reinforce the learning of chronology. So would student-made time lines and time charts in which events of one century or one period in one country can be related to the events of that period in another country. Exercises such as analyzing time belts, explaining the international date line and the World Calendar movement, and determining the date of Easter should prove valuable.

While we tend to concentrate on what can be called horizontal chronology, the tracing of developments through a long expanse of time, there is much to be said for the understanding of vertical chronology, the studying in depth of a narrow slice of time. A study of the biographies, journals, pictures, documents, and realia of a particular period can make that period come alive for the student investigator. Such a study of first-century

Rome, Elizabethan England, or New York in the 1870s can furnish the student with evidence of the customs, traditions, beliefs, and ideas which provide stability to society and civilization. Such an approach to history can also provide the student with an understanding of the work of the historian and the social scientist. The use of documents and journals should inevitably involve the evaluation of primary and secondary sources to verify facts, dates, and events. Thus, along with the greater understanding of time and chronology will come a greater feeling for the historical method of research.

Interpretation of Graphic Materials

The term "graphic materials" covers a wide range of instructional aids. Included in any reasonable definition would be the chalkboard, textbook illustrations, pictures (both still and moving, obtained from film, periodicals, television), graphs, charts, diagrams, cartoons, and other drawings and constructed materials (models and dioramas). Here we are concerned with the skills our students need to interpret various graphic materials and the methods by which the teacher of social studies can impart these skills.

Systematic instruction and practice in the use and interpretation of more sophisticated visual material are necessary in the classroom. As with many of the other skills, skill in interpreting graphic material is introduced in the elementary levels, so that the junior high school student has usually been exposed to many of the different graphic materials. The senior high school teacher's task, for the most part, is to reinforce and, if necessary, reteach and to provide sufficient opportunities for use and practice so that the student is able to perform the skill easily.

The graph is perhaps the most useful of devices for presenting data. The graph takes various forms, each with its particular strengths. Students should be instructed in the common elements of the various types of graphs: the title, the key, and the source. Every graph should have a title that indicates the purpose of the graphic representation. The key should clearly explain the meaning of the lines, symbols, intervals, shadings, and colors. The source should provide some indication of the reliability and recency of the information presented in the graph. Students must also be instructed to note first the overall import and intent of any graphic device, and then go on to examine its specific elements.

The following kinds of graphic materials are frequently found in world history:

1. **Simple line graphs.** These are best used to show trends or changes; this is probably the most frequently used graph. It connects points whose distance above the base line and to the sides represents comparative values. This kind of graph can represent data with the greatest accuracy. It is used for charting temperature changes during a month, the daily receipt at the customs house over a period of time, the position of the final standing of a ball team in the league over a period of years, and so on. Line graphs can show two or more related sets of data on the same graph by using two or more kinds of lines on the graph. This is fine for showing income and outgo, temperature and rainfall, exports and imports, and so on.

2. **Bar graph.** This graph, basically a variation of the line graph, comes in a great variety of forms. It can be horizontal or vertical; it can be shaded, colored, hachured; it can be separated or connected. Bar graphs are readily understood by students and are easily constructed.

3. **Circle or pie graphs.** These are excellent to represent percentages of a whole, the distribution of the tax dollar, the source of government income, the percentage of casualties in World War I by nationality, and so on. Here again, different colorings and shadings can be used; although the message of the circle or pie graph is usually quite clear without decorations. A variation that combines the bar graph and the pie or circle graph is the 100 per cent bar graph. Here each bar is the same size, but the extent of internal separations indicates the comparative percentage of the whole.

4. **Other graphs.** While the graphs described above are the usual forms used, there are as many kinds of graphs as there are creative minds. The comparative density of population of the United States and India could be presented on a pie graph as the percentages of a whole, on a 100 per cent

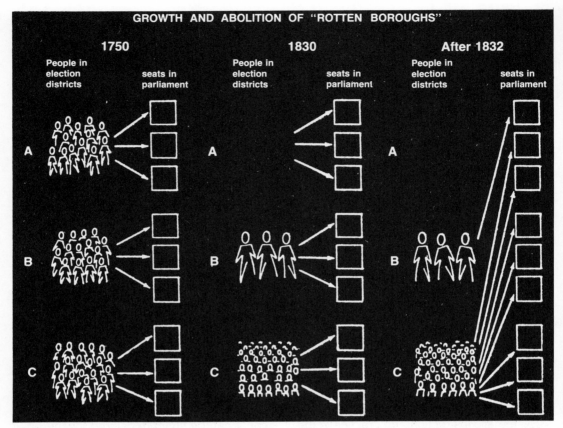

GROWTH AND ABOLITION OF "ROTTEN BOROUGHS"

bar graph again as the percentages of the whole, or on a vertical or horizontal bar graph.

Different geometric forms can be used to show comparative size. Differing sizes of squares in proportion to the data to be presented can show comparative population or school expenditure per capita, or value of resources. Triangles, circles, and other geometric figures can be used in similar fashion.

5. **Pictographs.** Based on the graph but using pictures, the pictograph is highly motivating and very simple and effective. The pictures may be cut out of a newspaper or drawn by hand. With each picture representing a certain number of tons, people, dollars, books, or whatever is being measured, the pictograph takes the place of the bar or line or pie in the usual graph (see above).

6. **Statistical charts or tables.** Graphs are usually based on a compilation of statistics that can be expressed in the form of a chart or statistical table. Students should be trained to interpret tables and charts and not to skip over them in their reading. Student assignments to gather information for charts and student projects to create graphs and pictographs from the charts should be an integral part of the instructional process. Just as students should read textbooks and supplementary materials and view and listen to films, pictures, and recordings with a critical eye and ear, so too should they learn to evaluate statistics in charts, tables, and graphs. What trends do the pictures indicate? Are there distortions in the way the graph is arranged—vertical distortion, horizontal distortion? Is the source of the material reliable? Is it up-to-date? What other sources are available to verify or contradict these statistics? What biases have crept into the selection of the information in the graph or chart or table? Students must be trained to ask such questions automatically, and this can be accomplished only by providing a sound program of instruction with

ample opportunity for practice and reinforcement of skills.

7. **Cartoons.** The cartoon can be used for various purposes during a lesson. Because of the impact of modern mass media of communication, it is particularly important that students be taught to be discriminating in their appreciation of editorial and news cartoons. They must learn to interpret political and social cartoons and to recognize the viewpoints expressed in them.

Cartoons may be obtained from newspapers and periodicals and can be duplicated in various ways so that each member of the class can have a copy. Two groups of questions can then be asked, one for test purposes, and the other designed to stimulate class discussion. If the cartoon is timely, and if it deals with a controversial subject, it can provide an excellent means of motivating students to have a meaningful discussion.

7

World History: Reading, Writing, Discussing

Although by now he is accustomed to teaching under the observation of his college supervisor and cooperating teacher, Mr. Loomis, a student teacher from State College, is unusually nervous. Despite every effort to retain his composure, he finds himself perspiring and his voice cracking.

He starts out well enough with his world history class, a group of low-ability students (median I.Q. 90; average reading retardation more than two years). To begin his lesson on the nature of the Commercial Revolution of the fifteenth and sixteenth centuries, he has brought to class tea, coffee, chocolate, a lemon, orange, banana, and a potato. He asks, "If I invited you to dine on a meal including the foods I have here, you would probably not regard it as a particularly good meal. Yet four hundred and fifty years ago, Europeans regarded such foods as real luxuries. How do you explain this? Miriam?"

Miriam: Maybe most of the people in those days couldn't afford this kind of food.

Alfred: Yeah, and only rich people could have it.

Mr. Loomis: But why would only rich people be able to have food we consider ordinary?

Salvatore: Maybe Europeans hardly knew about foods like these?

Mr. Loomis: Right you are. Most of these foods came from India and the Middle East (*pointing to the appropriate areas of the map*) and some from the New World in Mexico and South America. Why should the introduction of new foods and new fabrics interest men who study history?

Archie: New foods and new fabrics change the lives of people—the way they dress and the way they do things.

Claire: And women wear new styles, and even the furniture they have in their house changes.

Mr. Loomis: So great are the changes that new products can bring about that we sometimes describe such changes as a revolution. What's a revolution? Ted?

Ted: A revolution is a war or something.

Mr. Loomis: Well, a revolution is often a war, but if people start drinking coffee when they didn't do so before, it's hardly a war but it may be *revolutionary*. (*He writes the word on the board*.) Why?

Ted: Well, if it's not a war, then a revolution is a sudden change that made entirely new conditions for people to live with.

Mr. Loomis: Very good. What should we try to find out then as we study the new foods and goods that were introduced into Europe?

Maxine: We could find out how new products changed the lives of Europeans.

Mr. Loomis: That's excellent, Maxine, but what word might be substituted for the word change?

Maxine: Maybe "revolutioned"?

Mr. Loomis: Let's put it on the board this way: "How did new products revolutionize people's lives?" (*He writes on the board. He then distributes a reading passage and explains slowly*.) In this passage we will see how fast you read and how much you understand. When I say "Begin," start reading, and when I say "Stop," look up. Then count the words you read. Notice that the end of each paragraph has the number of words in it, so you don't have to count from the beginning. Write the number of words you read on a sheet of notebook paper, and on the same sheet begin answering the five questions that you find below the selection.

At his signal, the class begins to read. After he calls out, "Stop reading, and count the number of words you have completed at this time," Mr. Loomis asks the students to begin answering the questions. As they do so, he walks about, noting

55

the number of words completed and how the questions are being answered. It is at this time that his voice cracks as he tries to help individual students. Mr. Loomis is beset with doubts. What will the supervisor think? After all, this is a lesson in world history, not English. Isn't the silence oppressive? Relieved, he notices that after about fifteen minutes most of the students have completed the answers to the questions and that he can proceed to a discussion based on those answers. This he does until a minute or so before the bell is due to ring. Then he summarizes the lesson through effective questioning.

The Commercial Revolution led to a radical change in European taste. The better middle-class houses were not considered comfortable without glass windows, wooden or tiled roofs, carpets and rugs, and upholstered furniture. The cheapening of cotton and linen cloth made possible the introduction of more comfortable clothing. Furs were especially a symbol of wealth and social rank. The use of silk was considerably increased. (65 words)

The range of foods was greatly enlarged. Probably the most important food product introduced into Europe was the potato. Sugar was first extensively introduced at this time. With the discovery of sugar cane, particularly in the West Indies, sugar came to be used in increasing quantities. Important tropical fruits were now brought into Europe for the first time in greater quantities than before. Among these were oranges, pineapples, bananas, and lemons. Several new varieties of fowl were introduced, particularly the turkey from Mexico. (148 words)

Probably the new beverages did more than the foods and house furnishings to alter the pattern of social contact in Europe. The Dutch in the East Indies learned tea drinking from the Chinese and introduced it into Europe in the seventeenth century. Within a hundred years it became an important commodity of world trade. Europeans discovered the virtues of coffee through contact with Arabia at the close of the Middle Ages. Nearly all the coffee consumed in Europe until the close of the seventeenth century came from this area. In the following century the Dutch transplanted the industry to their East Indian lands. The Portuguese carried it to Brazil. The establishment of coffee houses began a new chapter in the social life of Europe. (272 words)[1]

Mr. Loomis was unnecessarily concerned about how his supervisor would react to his lesson. Not only was he told that he had taught a superior lesson, but that taking time to diagnose reading difficulties and develop reading skills was a major responsibility of the world history teacher.

[1]Adapted from Harry Elmer Barnes, *The History of Western Civilization*, Volume II, New York: Harcourt Brace, Inc., 1935.

Building Vocabulary

In order to understand world history, a student must have an adequate grasp of the vocabulary related to it. Probably no subject has a vocabulary that is more difficult for average and slow students to grasp. In addition, in many world history texts the learner is confronted with a specialized vocabulary, thus adding to the general frustration of the poorer student. Often students have but the vaguest notion of the meaning of imperialism, nationalism, democracy, republicanism, internationalism, or such terms as international anarchy, collective security, alliance, arbitration. Moreover, these terms are used in a variety of ways, depending on the sentence and the general frame of reference. Students are beset with difficulties when common English words are used with the peculiar shades of meaning that they often assume in world history—neutral or neutrality, belligerent, aggressor or aggressive, and mobilization. World history is also filled with foreign terms such as *Anschluss, apartheid, Ausgleich, blitzkrieg, irredenta, Lebensraum*, and difficult geographic place names and technical terms such as bay, peninsula, island, inlet, delta, and harbor. Terms denoting a point of view, such as right, left, center, progressive, liberal, reactionary, conservative, radical, revolutionary, are ambiguous and understandably confusing. Beyond this, there are those whose names have a peculiar ring and a more peculiar spelling: Hammurabi, Euripides, Macapagal, Khrushchev, Brezhnev, Sadat, Peres, Mao Tse-tung.

All teachers must be aware of the formidable difficulties the vocabulary of world history presents to slow and superior students alike, although obviously the nature of these difficulties and their levels will vary considerably.

The following are some ways of meeting the problem of a specialized vocabulary in world history:

1. **In giving the homework assignment, anticipate vocabulary difficulties.** Call new words to the attention of the class and discuss those words briefly.

2. **Have students keep a vocabulary list in their notebooks.** Here they should list terms that require definition, together with their meanings and perhaps an appropriate illustrative sentence.

3. **While teaching, jot down strange names and terms on the board, to clarify their meanings and spellings and to furnish visual reinforcement.** Thus, if the teacher or a student refers to Josef Vissarionovich Dzhugashvili (Stalin), write it on the board so that students can see the name and perhaps learn how to spell it.

4. **On a more formal basis, set aside a specific place on the chalkboard or bulletin board for a vocabulary list.** Here you list those new vocabulary words which have been developed during the lesson, or perhaps even leave the list on long enough so that the terms accumulate over a week or more.

5. **Sometimes the development of vo-**

cabulary **is so vital to an understanding of a particular subject that special lessons are required.** Thus, with even good classes it would not be amiss to develop with them the meaning of right, left, center, conservative, radical, liberal, reactionary. The origin of these terms, their use as a description of a political point of view and the cautions that must be observed in using them as party designations, must be impressed upon the class.

6. **Where classes are especially slow in learning, special reading assignments in which word meanings are developed in class are especially appropriate, using a technique similar to that used by Mr. Loomis.** With slow classes it is also important to provide students with a background that gives meaning to words. Trips, films, and filmstrips will serve as points of departure for the development of relevant vocabulary.

Developing Reading Comprehension

"Some books are to be tasted, others to be swallowed, and some few to be chewed and digested," said Francis Bacon. Because books serve different purposes, students must learn to read for different purposes as well. The skills required of them will vary. Every teacher must teach how to match the reading skills with the job to be done, but this is particularly important for the teacher of world history.

Foremost among the comprehension skills is the ability to get the main thought from a particular paragraph or passage. In slow learning classes especially, the teacher must allow ample opportunity for reading both in class and, if possible, at home, so that students learn to summarize main thoughts in their own words. In class, students should read a selection from the text and then give the main thought, which, in turn, is summarized on the blackboard by the teacher or by the students. If such an exercise is assigned as homework, it should be reviewed in class.

When asking students to develop the main thought, the teacher should caution them to use their own words. The main thought should not be permitted to stand in isolation, but should be applied to the unit being studied or to the lesson for the day.

As we read above, Mr. Loomis found the silence oppressive during that interlude in which he asked the class to read. He was uneasy because there seemed to be so little student or teacher activity. Mr. Loomis had reason for apprehension, but he was right in what he decided to do and how he did it. Reading is a very fine form of student activity, but the teacher must be active too. The teacher's activity consists, first, in planning a lesson in which the reading assignment is motivated and the class is made ready for the reading that is to follow. "Reading readiness" is a term often associated with early childhood education, but it is not merely confined to one state of instruction. It means that for each lesson in reading, in school or at home, the class must be prepared in advance; a purpose for reading must be identified, and the chief obstacles to reading with a substantial measure of comprehension must be cleared away.

When a class is reading silently, the teacher should take that opportunity to provide for individual differences. This can be done by helping students who seem to be having special reading problems by having them read aloud, by asking them to state the main thought found in a paragraph, or by assisting them with difficult vocabulary. In addition, the teacher must plan a follow-up activity after the class has read for a time in silence. This may be a summary or an application of the main thoughts to the content of world history.

Getting the main thought from the printed page is not the only skill of reading comprehension that must be developed. Students must be taught to read rapidly, to skim, if necessary, in order to obtain quickly details that are pertinent to the topic under discussion. Skimming is more than casually glancing over the paragraph; it involves rapid reading with a specific end in view. Sometimes the end is simply to gain a general idea of the contents of the paragraph, or more likely to isolate specific facts. For example, a student should be able to skim an appropriate paragraph in his text and quickly find the answer to such questions as "Who wrote the Magna Carta?" "When was it written?" and perhaps even its chief provisions. These data can be written on the board quickly by the teacher or, even better, by a student secretary; and they can be used as a springboard for a significant discussion based on such questions as "Why has Magna Carta become valued as a basic guarantee of the liberties of free people?" Or "Wherein did Magna Carta fall short of our concept of civil liberties?" Again, these facts gleaned from the skill of skimming for details should not be allowed to stand in isolation, but should be incorporated into the broader picture, contributing toward the realization of the lesson's aim.

Casual reading must be distinguished from intensive study. The student should realize that the best way to study a particular topic intensively is to consider all the separate elements included under our general term "reading comprehension." Thus, a student might (1) define vocabulary words in the topic he or she wishes to study, (2) summarize the main thoughts in the pages he or she is reading, (3) skim the paragraph or page for specific details, and (4) apply these thoughts and facts to the questions assigned.

Developing Writing Skills

In his *Essay on Criticism*, Alexander Pope wrote:

> True ease in writing comes from art, not chance,
> As those move easiest who have learn'd to dance.

True ease in writing is acquired only through constant practice. By providing ample opportunities to write in world history courses, teachers can help their students to write more effectively and to express themselves both articulately and accurately.

The world history teacher, however, can make a real contribution toward the development of writing skills:

1. **In assigning homework, ask that extended answers be given to carefully thought-out essay questions.** These should be evaluated from time to time by the class as a whole. Answers can be read aloud in class, or students can exchange papers. Some answers can be reproduced on the board. Probably the best way is to insert a number of representative answers in the opaque or overhead projector, to be read from the screen by the class. Among the items the class might discuss are (a) effectiveness of organization, (b) accuracy of content, (c) English usage.

2. **Provide ample opportunity for answering essay questions on examinations, and have the class evaluate the answers.**

3. **Assign term papers or compositions related to a unit or lesson.** The term paper can make a valuable contribution to the world history program, but a number of precautions must be kept in mind when using it. Several short papers are usually preferable to one long one. A short paper requires that the student delimit the topic more carefully; the teacher is given more time to evaluate the papers; and, when several short papers are to be assigned, improvement from one paper to the next can be noted. Students must be taught how to document their reports, how to provide a bibliography, how to use quotations, and when and to whom to give credit for words and ideas.

4. **If a term paper is worth assigning, certainly it should be graded with a reasonable degree of care.** For a student to have his paper returned only with a letter grade or with an illegible comment on the title page is certainly a disappointment. If at all possible, individual conferences with each student should be organized. If it is not possible to have such a conference with all students, then it is better to select a few whose papers require individual help and meet with them to upgrade their written work. On occasion, time may be taken when the papers are returned to have the students report briefly on their research, the difficulties they had, and the additional research that might be done by more serious or advanced scholars in the same field.

Informal Discussion in World History

Student-led discussions have a very real place in the world history classroom. They provide opportunities for varying lessons and they lend an element of zest to the teaching of world history. They provide effective means by which current controversial issues can be aired and conflicting interpretations of historical episodes explored.

The student chairperson of an informal discussion has a number of responsibilities and must be coached for the role he or she is to play. Because the opportunity to serve as student chairperson should be rotated among as many students as possible, the teacher should choose the chairperson, rather than have the class make the choice.

Once the topic and the chairperson have been identified, the teacher and the chairperson should have a conference or two, during which the chair's role should be defined, the issues involved in the topic clarified, and any illustrative material evaluated. The following are some of the responsibilities that the teacher should explain to a student chairperson:

- **The chair restates the topic or problem, writes it on the board, and establishes the climate in which the informal discussion can proceed.**
- **The chair makes an effort to be thoroughly prepared on the topic.** He or she has available relevant statistics, quotations, and opinions of experts which he or she introduces from time to time.
- **The chair allows substantial freedom of student response but keeps the discussion relevant to the topic.**
- **The chair does not allow the discussion to become dominated by a few.** Instead, leadership talents are exercised by the chair to call on nonparticipants.
- **The chair does not monopolize the discussion.** Although he or she may have more information on a given topic than any one member of the class, he or she is unlikely to have more information than the group as a whole, and it is his or her responsibility to bring as much of this information out into the open as possible.
- **The chair is aware of time limitations, and toward the end of the discussion summarizes, perhaps by calling on one or two students, or perhaps doing it by himself or herself, restating the main points.** These may be noted on the blackboard and perhaps copied by the students into their notebooks.

Student-led discussions are highly desirable, and many teachers have used them to good advantage. For example, some teachers use a student chairperson to conduct a five-minute review of the previous day's lesson. Others use a student chairperson to begin each day's work, with a review or with some other activity, whenever unavoidable circumstances make them a few minutes late for the beginning of the period. A well trained class can often accomplish a good deal during the first few minutes, even when the teacher is out of the room—perhaps, because of it!

The responsibility placed on a student to conduct an informal discussion is rather great, and relatively few students have the leadership capacities that such discussion requires. However, because it is desirable to develop at least some of the qualities of leadership in all our students, there has been a growing tendency to use groups or committees of students, rather than a single student chairperson.

The Panel

A panel consists of a group of from five to seven interested students who select a moderator or chairperson from among themselves and discuss an agreed-upon problem. This kind of discussion is informal, but issues should be developed and dilemmas making a decision elusive should be revealed. No member makes a report, although the chairperson may introduce the topic and explain why a problem exists and why the topic was chosen.

Members of the panel should meet among themselves and with the teacher to discuss the general format and the responsibilities of each panelist. An outline and a time allotment may also be drawn up. In particular, time should be allowed for class participation, with the chairperson usually calling for questions and looking for answers from panel members, as well as from other class members.

In their *Handbook of Group Discussion*, Russell Wagner and Carroll Arnold caution that while preparation is imperative, the topic should not be rehearsed or discussed ahead of time. They say that too often the preparation is so thorough that the discussion itself loses its spontaneity and assumes an air of stageyness.[2] However, in-

[2]Russell Wagner and Carroll Arnold, *Handbook of Group Discussion*. Boston: Houghton Mifflin Company, 1950, p. 168.

experienced discussants may wish to prepare an outline in advance.

Wagner and Arnold suggest, "With. . .an
outline in mind (but not in *hand*!), a public
discussion should feel more free, less har-
ried, and more confident of its ability to cover the subject in the allotted time. The outline should never be viewed as a blueprint
or stencil which actual discussion must du-
plicate exactly. It should be simple, short,
and flexible."[3]

The Round Table

A round table discussion is even more informal than a panel discussion. It usually involves fewer than five people, with a less
structured discussion than in the panel. In
both panel and round table discussions, it is
best if students actually do sit around a
round table or in some fashion that encourages intimate and informal exchange of
views. They should be in a position where
they can face the audience as well as one
another, but their remarks should be addressed, initially at least, to one another (in
voices loud enough for all to hear), rather
than to the classroom audience.

The Symposium

Approximately the same number of students participate in a symposium as in a
panel. However, here each participant se-
lects a particular aspect of the topic under
consideration and prepares a brief but formal statement or talk on it. The symposium
chairperson has the responsibility of stating
the topic and its significance, of introducing
each speaker, and of relating one speaker's
remarks to those of another.

Although the symposium obviously differs
from the panel, in the world history classroom the two terms have been used inter-
changeably. The panel in the world history
class is often in the form of prepared remarks. Too often the spontaneous thinking
aloud that should be characteristic of a panel is lacking. It is an excellent procedure to
distinguish between the two techniques for
the class so that the proper format may be
chosen for every situation.

The Forum

A forum is a public discussion in which
the audience is directly invited to partici-
[3]*Ibid.*, p. 169.

pate. The panel, round table, or symposium
generally yield toward the end of the session to audience participation. In this sense,
they come to resemble a forum. When this
happens, the attitude and responsibilities of
the participating members must change,
particularly those of the chairperson. The
chairperson must encourage questions, invite panel or symposium members to answer, and provide orderly leadership over
the larger group. In a student-led discussion
in world history, even in one that is technical
in nature, the remaining members of the
class are almost always invited to participate. Indeed, the chairperson must allow
time for them to do so; and the teacher must
give an assignment in the form of readings
so that class members are prepared to answer and ask questions.

The Debate

In world history discussion, a debate is
any formal exchange of opposing views.
Thus, a discussion based on the topic "Re-
solved: The United States should withdraw
from its bases in Turkey" may be regarded
as an informal debate since opposing views
are being presented, usually with one or two
persons taking the affirmative side and the
same number taking the negative side.

The formal debate is not generally encouraged in the world history classroom,
since the object of a formal debate is to win,
while the object of an informal classroom
presentation of opposing views is to contribute to a resolution of the difficulty and/or to
enlighten the audience concerning the issues at stake. While a formal debate may
yield these extra dividends, an informal one
makes these the heart of the discussion.

The Report

Theorists on education, from Plato to
Dewey, have been concerned about the
role of the individual in his or her relation to
society. The problem was and remains how
to reconcile the need for individual expression and individual initiative with the
needs for communal cooperation. Rousseau isolated Émile from society in order
to develop and encourage his natural intellectual growth as an individual. This is neither possible nor desirable in the modern
classroom, but the individual report provides one way of utilizing the natural and

spontaneous interests of students and of capitalizing on their emotional and intellectual capacities.

Thus, we ask students to report in order to provide outlets for their creativity and originality. For example, what could be more rewarding for all concerned than for a young stamp collector to report on the stamps issued by the Weimar Republic to provide the group with some insight into the inflationary problems of postwar Germany? What could be more effective than having a student interested in music report on the music of Latin America when that region is being studied? How desirable it is to ask a bright student, bored by class routine, to do a brief research paper on the Russo-Japanese War from the Japanese, Russian, or American point of view, and to ask the student to report orally on the results of the research. Individual reports on trips students have taken, books they have read, persons they have met, and unusual but pertinent experiences they have had are all techniques of encouraging and utilizing individual interests and abilities.

Evaluating Group Discussions and Oral Reports

Evaluation involves attempts to answer such questions as "How well did we do?" "How efficient were our routines and procedures?" "What did we learn?" "Were our materials effectively used?" "How should we proceed?" Evaluation of student-led discussions and oral reports should be a process of self-evaluation with a view toward self-improvement.

Evaluating a discussion or report means not only identifying its good points, but also recognizing frankly that time may have been wasted, that panelists, reporters, or the class as a whole may have been unprepared, that the topic might have been studied more expeditiously some other way, that important materials were neglected, that significant content was omitted, or that the attitude and/or decorum of the class or the discussants was not as it should have been.

There is a danger, however, that such discussions may become unduly discursive and insufficiently critical because students may not want to criticize their classmates' work. On the other hand, criticism may be

unduly harsh, and sensitive students may be unnecessarily hurt. Moreover, this procedure is likely to be too time-consuming to be used after every report or group discussion. A checklist for group discussions and oral reports may help to keep evaluation procedures efficient.

Checklist for Group Discussion and Oral Reports

Content and Materials

1. Was the topic appropriate?
2. Was the topic appropriately worded?
3. Were the discussion leaders well prepared?
4. Was the discussion based on reliable sources?
5. Was the content developed with adequate insight and understanding?
6. Did the class seem to learn from the discussion?
7. Did a spirit of free inquiry seem to prevail?
8. Was there evidence of an objective pursuit of truth?
9. Were the discussion leaders free of prejudice?
10. Was there a general respect for facts?

Presentation

1. Was the discussion spontaneous though planned?
2. Did the discussion leaders think aloud?
3. Were the speakers enthusiastic?
4. Did the speakers express themselves effectively?
5. Did each participant know what was expected of him or her?
6. Did the chairperson fulfill the role well?
7. Did the class participate effectively?
8. Was the blackboard used appropriately?
9. Were illustrative materials, if any, used effectively?

Procedures and Routines

1. Did the group and class get started promptly?
2. Was the class attentive to the discussion?
3. Was the discussion properly timed to allow for a brief introduction, adequate de-

velopment of the topic, and a brief summary?

4. Did the group choose an appropriate format for the discussion?

5. Were the seating arrangements of discussants and class conducive to effective discussion?

The above checklist is intended mainly for discussion, but with some modifications it can also be applied to individual oral reports.

Thomas Babington Macaulay aptly described discussion when he said, "Men are never so likely to settle a question rightly as when they discuss it freely." In this spirit, formal and informal discussion and oral students reports, when prudently used, are among the more valuable techniques of world history instruction.

1492 1629 1914 1929 1972 1776 1812 1877 1863 1959 1941 3

8

World History: Its Mastery

Sample Questions from a World History Examination

Directions: Write all your answers on the paper provided; do NOT write on this paper.

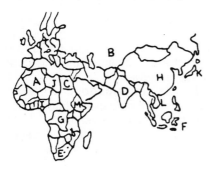

PART I: SHORT ANSWER

I. **Map Question:** On your answer paper next to the appropriate number for each question, write the LETTER of the place on the map which best locates the place described.

1. This nation has withdrawn from the Commonwealth of Nations because of criticism of its racial policies.
2. This nation had a long and bloody revolution before winning independence from France.

II. **Multiple Choice:** On your answer paper, write the LETTER of the word or phrase that best completes each of the following:

1. One of the major problems facing the new nations of Africa is (a) admission to the United Nations; (b) establishing a united defense force; (c) change from tribal to national loyalty; (d) the influence of European countries.
2. The development of Arab nationalism has led to (a) hostility toward Israel; (b) an alliance against communism; (c) greater investments by England and France; (d) pooling of natural resources of all Arab nations.

III. **Identification:** From the names listed below, on your answer paper write the LETTER in front of the name that best fits each description.
a. Cecil Rhodes   g. Gamal Nasser
b. David Ben-Gurion   h. Mohandas Gandhi
c. Chiang Kai-shek   i. Mao Tse-tung
d. Lord Balfour   j. Robert Clive
e. Achmed Sukarno   k. Moise Tshombe
f. Hendrik Verwoerd   l. Ho Chi Minh

1. I have recently nationalized American oil interests in Indonesia.
2. It was my declaration that favored the creation of a Jewish homeland in Palestine.

IV. **Selection:** On your answer paper, write the LETTER of the item in each of the following groups which *does not belong* to the group.

1. Three principles of Sun Yat-sen: (a) democracy; (b) livelihood; (c) nationalism; (d) imperialism.
2. Strategic points on Britain's "lifeline to India": (a) Malta; (b) Suez Canal; (c) Gibraltar; (d) Hong Kong.

PART II: ESSAY QUESTIONS

Purposes of Testing

"Tests make us pale," sang medieval students, and their words find an echo among today's youth when they are subjected to tests of which the above is but one example. At the very outset, it is well to remember that evaluation in world history includes more than just testing. It includes as well all the evidence the world history teacher is able to gather about a student through conversations, interviews, class discussions, class participation, board work, homework, and the written reports handed in from time to time, such as term papers and book reports. Evaluation seeks to determine personality development, as well as intellectual growth as measured by a student's relative standing in the class or group, and, perhaps more important, in terms of his own progress and capacity. It seeks to determine, in part, the degree to which a student is achieving success in terms of his own goals and aspirations. While tests attempt to provide an objective, quantitative measure of student progress, evaluation is a subjective, nonquantitative judgment of a student by his or her teacher.

Despite the fact that evaluation includes measurable as well as non-measurable factors, the former, rather than the latter, for better or worse, probably plays the greater role in the evaluation process. Because tests play so significant a role in the process of education, teachers at all levels are constantly making an effort to determine whether the tests they have chosen or prepared are: valid (Do they measure what they are supposed to measure?); reliable (Do they yield consistent results?); objective (Do they treat all students alike?). At Harvard University, professors were asked to evaluate the necessity and merits of the tests they gave to undergraduates. The answers they gave were revealing in that they suggested some of the purposes for which tests are given. A test was variously described as a "silent teacher," as a "teaching tool in its own right," and as "a device for simplifying academic bookkeeping."[1]

In view of these descriptions and some of the statements we have already made, the purposes of testing in world history may be conveniently summarized as follows:

The Test as a Silent Teacher

1. **To summarize units of work.** Properly constructed tests should help to summarize the highlights of what has been studied and the significant data and concepts that have emerged.

2. **To fix information.** A well constructed test will help clinch information and fix specific data in the students' minds by showing them a relationship between what they have studied and some new or unexpected development.

3. **To provide a basis for remedial work.** A thoughtfully interpreted test will help the teacher prepare a series of lessons designed to improve the skills and understanding of those students whose test results indicate they need help. Tests likewise help in grouping students based on measured ability and on remedial needs.

4. **To determine the effectiveness of teaching.** Tests can reveal to teachers the success of their efforts and wherein their procedures may require modification.

5. **To determine curriculum improvement.** Properly regarded and interpreted, the test may point out areas of the curriculum that require expansion or contraction.

---

[1]*The New York Times*. December 3, 1963.

The Test as a Means of Academic Bookkeeping

1. **To determine a student's standing.** Tests are probably the chief determinant of a student's grade and therefore of his or her standing in the class.

2. **To measure a student's progress.** Properly prepared, tests will reveal how much intellectual growth a student has achieved since he or she was last tested and how much progress has been made in relation to others in the class.

3. **To furnish a basis for conferences.** Few devices are quite so valuable in forming a convenient point of departure for a conference with the student or with parents or guidance counselors than the results he or she obtained on a given examination.

4. **To furnish a measure of objectivity in marking.** Since we have a responsibility not to permit our subjective judgment and unconscious bias to form the total basis for grading students, tests form a convenient way of providing some objective yardstick by which students' marks may be determined.

A test, then, is both a tool of teaching and a tool of evaluation. It is an instrument by which we measure the effectiveness of our teaching and our students' learning. It helps us to diagnose our students' difficulties and evaluate the merits of our curriculum.

Types of Test Questions

The validity of any test is only as good as the questions it asks. In ancient China, for example, to recruit outstanding officials for government service, candidates were asked to compose a poem on "The sound of the oars and the green of the hills and water," or to write a composition on the theme "To possess ability, and yet to ask of those who do not, to know much and yet inquire of those who know little, to possess and yet appear not to possess, to be full and yet appear empty."[2] How would American students like to try their hand at these?

Because questions such as these failed to measure adequately those qualities required for effective government service, the Chinese bureaucracy in time became so rigid and formal in its thinking and so utterly lacking in new ideas and originality that eventually China was unable to respond to the challenges offered by changing times and hostile neighbors. While the tests teachers give may have no such dire results, the fact is that to the extent that their questions fail to measure the aims of world history, they will have no way of knowing whether the goals they have so conscientiously sought have indeed been met. To the extent that their questions fail to measure the desirable outcomes of world history instruction, such questions impose a straitjacket on the curriculum, inhibitions on the students, and restraints on innovations in the classroom. Ineffective testing resulting from ill-conceived questioning, instead of becoming one of many instruments of effective teaching and proper evaluation, becomes merely an obstacle course over whose hurdles students may learn to leap— but perhaps without learning anything of lasting value.

By and large, two broad types of questions are available for us: the essay question and the short-answer question. The essay question, as its name tells us, usually calls for the student to provide an extended answer, usually written in continuous dis-

[2]Will Durant, *Our Oriental Heritage.* New York: Simon and Schuster, 1942, p. 801.

course. It allows the students to express their thoughts freely and to organize them as they see fit. Thus, it attempts to encourage and evaluate such intangible qualities as creativity and originality, as well as growth in ability to select data and draw pertinent conclusions based on the data.

The short-answer question usually requires the student to answer by supplying or selecting the word or letter which properly answers the question. Short-answer questions include four broad categories: the completion type, the true-false question, the matching question, and the multiple-choice question. Other short answer questions are modifications of these basic types, as we shall see. These questions are widely used because of the ease in scoring and because they treat all candidates alike without permitting the subjective judgment of the examiner to enter into the final results. However, to say that these are "objective" questions, as is so often done, is not entirely accurate, for frequently the bias of the examiner may be found in the questions selected, the wording or emphasis given, and, above all, in the answers accepted as correct.

Writing a good test is a painful process, and there is no magic wand by which the pain can be made to disappear. We do propose, however, to discuss each of the varieties of questions at some length, and to make some suggestions as to how teachers can develop skill in preparing them.

Essay Questions

To write a good essay question is no easy matter, but following a number of rules will help teachers to do so:

1. **Be sure that the essay question calls for the student to do something that cannot be evaluated in any other way.** Thus, "List the five most important financial centers of the world" is not an essay question because it asks for information that could be tested more effectively through short-answer questions.

2. **A good essay question tells something to the student as well as asks something.** Thus, "In *The Rise of the West* by William H. McNeill may be found the following statement: 'The loss to human cul-

ture in the Spanish extirpation (destruction) of the American Indian civilization does not seem very great. Over centuries and millennia who can say what might have arisen? But in 1500 A.D., the actual achievements of the New World were trifling as compared to those of the old.' To what extent would you agree or disagree with this statement?"

3. **Suggest an organization or a framework for the answer required.** A question such as "Write an essay on the subject of nationalism" is not without its merits, especially for advanced classes. But its defect is that it offers so much opportunity for pupils' responses that the pupil does not know how much to write or what to emphasize for a perfect score. Because so many facets of nationalism may legitimately be discussed, the answers would not be at all comparable. A better question on nationalism would be: "Show how each of the following contributed to the growth of nationalism in the country indicated: (a) Facing a common enemy—the United States during the eighteenth century; (b) Geographic factors—Italy during the nineteenth century; (c) Traditions—India during the twentieth century." In this question, notice also that because an extended answer was required, the question was broken down into several parts. This encourages comparability of answers and greater objectivity in determining the worth of the answer. The question also suggests the breadth and depth expected of the student's answer.

4. **Try to ensure an adequate sampling by providing for a wide variety of activities and by drawing from each area of the content to be tested.**

5. **Teach students how to answer an essay question.** Too often teachers assume that students should know how to write answers to their questions. But such is not the case. Time should be taken to teach specifically the skills required to do such things as organize, compare, contrast, evaluate, enumerate, cite, discuss, describe, explain, and define.

Grading an essay paper requires some care and forethought. As we have already implied, structure the essay question in such a manner that the answers received are at least roughly comparable, and word them in such a way that students know approximately what they must do to obtain a perfect score. Try not looking at the names on the papers to insure impartiality and to eliminate a possible halo effect—that is, the tendency to mark down those students teachers may dislike or have reason to believe are not doing well, or to mark up those whose engaging personalities may lead them to believe that they are doing quite well. In some cases it may be possible to assign numbers to the students. In other cases, have the students write their names upside down, or at the foot of the page, so that the name of the student is not immediately conspicuous to the teacher's eye.

Before beginning to grade the papers, teachers should make up a model answer of the essential facts they expect to find in the answers of the papers they are to grade. Then they should read a few of the students' papers without assigning any grade to them, just to get an idea of the general level of the answers they can expect; and they can add to their model answer any pertinent information their students have used but which they did not include. Once they get going and begin assigning numerical values to the answers, they can read each paper relatively quickly, letting their eyes pick up the hard facts so that these are drawn to their attention. By reading rapidly and by reading the answers to the same question before they turn to another, they will be more likely to evaluate each paper in terms of the specifics provided and in terms of the comparable answers provided by others.

The task of grading essay answers is not an easy one; it is a chore heartily disliked by most teachers. Nevertheless, it is a task that cannot be prudently avoided or indifferently treated. However, because essay questions by themselves cannot furnish a completely impartial yardstick of student achievement, good tests in world history should contain both essay and short-answer questions.

Short-Answer Questions

Among the older forms of short-answer question is the completion type of question in which the student is asked to supply the name, term, or word which best completes the statement or answers the question. The completion question was long popular because it is deceptively simple to prepare and because it discourages guessing. Because a well constructed question was believed to measure effectively the information the student had actually retained over a period of time, the completion question was considered a desirable device with which to evaluate growth in specific knowledge.

Although the possible advantages of the completion question cannot be denied, the fact of the matter is that it has so many faults that today it is no longer so popular nor so acceptable as it once was. In world history we seek to measure growth in skills, attitudes, and reflective thinking; the completion question seems to measure only what the student has memorized the night before. Because it encourages only memorized responses, it also has a tendency to encourage teaching and work study habits which put a premium on memory responses, rather than upon creative thought.

Despite these serious drawbacks, the completion question continues to be used; and, properly constructed, it offers a desirable alternative to the more widely used matching or multiple-choice type of question, which we shall discuss shortly. The following rules can serve as guidelines for this testing technique:

- **Avoid language that permits the student to supply several reasonable answers.** Thus, "The author of *Mein Kampf* was __ __" could reasonably and correctly be answered by the student who writes "Adolf Hitler" as well as by the one who writes "A German" or even, perhaps, "a madman." Which answer should teachers accept?

- **To avoid this condition, it is sometimes better to ask a question, rather than to use an incomplete sentence or a sentence fragment.** Thus, "Who was the author of Mein Kampf? ____" might avoid the ambiguity that the incomplete sentence above suggests, although admittedly it does not eliminate it completely.

- **Textbook language should be avoided, as should the giving of any clues to the answer.** Thus, "That bacteria cause disease was discovered by

Louis _____" is poor because of the clue given by mention of the first name. Moreover, this question could be improved by asking "Who discovered that bacteria cause disease? _____." Another question which suggests the answer is "An _____ was the first person Columbus saw in the New World." The article "an" suggests that the missing word must begin with a vowel ("Indian"); and it is, therefore, an unnecessary and undesirable clue.

• **Make the blanks of equal length and place them uniformly on the page.** Thus, it is often better to place the blank at the beginning of the question so that all the answers appear in one place. This adds to ease of grading as well.

• **In preparing completion questions, avoid asking for unnecessary detail.** Be sure that the facts you want to elicit are worth requiring the student to commit to memory.

• **The briefer the answer you want the student to supply, the better; since this adds to the degree of objectivity you can achieve, and it reduces the possibility of logically correct answers but not the answer for which you were looking.**

One form of completion question that overcomes at least some of the difficulties encountered in its use is a story in which blanks are provided for the student to fill in the missing items. The following is an example of such a question:[3]

> Read the following selection and in the spaces provided below the paragraph write the term or name that best completes the paragraph:
>
> After World War I a new form of absolute government arose in the form of *1* ___. Because it had complete control over the minds of men and the machinery of government it has also been called *2* ___. In Russia it took the form of *3* ___; in Italy it took the form of *4* ___; and in Germany *5* ___. In Russia *6* ___ took advantage of his country's troubles to carry out the Revolution of 1971. In Italy *7* ___ made his March on Rome and soon became that country's Duce. In Germany, Hitler's early effort to overthrow the *8* ___ Republic failed. In jail he wrote *9* ___ and prepared for the day

---

[3]From Tests for *The Pageant of World History* by Gerald Leinwand. © Copyright 1962, 1966 by Allyn and Bacon, Inc. Reprinted by permission of Allyn and Bacon, Inc.

when he would seize power. The civil war in *10* ___ was called a "dress rehearsal" for World War II and there, too, democracy was defeated.

1. _____ 6. _____
2. _____ 7. _____
3. _____ 8. _____
4. _____ 9. _____
5. _____ 10. _____

In such a question there are ample opportunities available to students to use their intelligence and to figure out the answers for themselves without relying entirely on rote memory responses. (Memory responses are occasionally desirable; an over-concentration on them, however, is objectionable.)

The True-False Question

The true-false question, like the completion question, has been widely used by teachers over the years. Its advantages are that it is simple to grade and that, in marking at least, the student is treated with impartiality. By and large, however, the true-false question has a number of serious shortcomings, not the least of which is the encouragement it gives to guessing. Moreover, like the completion question, it is deceptively simple in appearance but difficult to write. That is, it is extremely difficult to write a clear, unambiguous statement that would be true or false under all circumstances and in every way.

Nevertheless, because true-false questions do open another avenue for questioning in examinations, teachers often wish to use them. Again, there are a number of rules which, if carefully observed, will help teachers write a better test item of the true-false variety. Since many of the rules applying to completion questions are relevant also for true-false questions, they need not be repeated at length here. It is sufficient to state that ambiguous statements must be avoided, as should the language of the textbook. Teachers should be sure that only significant items are questioned, rather than relatively minor details. Among the rules for the effective preparation of valid true-false questions, the following are the more significant:

• **Be sure to base the question on a statement that is entirely true or entirely false without exception.**

- **Be sure that the item being tested is central to the question, and that the question is not being used merely to trap the student.**
- **Avoid giving the question away with such absolute qualifiers as "all," "none," "never," "always."** Thus, "All workers are members of labor unions"; or "A depression always follows a war." In both cases the safe and obviously correct answer is false.
- **On the other hand, avoid trapping the student by using negatives or tricks of any kind.**

Although the true-false question has a number of inherent difficulties and serious shortcomings, the modified true-false question may be used to good advantage. One modification requires the student to correct those statements which he considers false. Another modification lends itself to the testing of skills in interpreting cartoons, statistics, charts, or reading passages, by providing a third alternative other than merely true or false. Examples of questions of these types follow:[4]

Indicate whether the following statements about the United Nations are TRUE or FALSE. If the statement is FALSE, rewrite it to make it true.

1. Every member of the Security Council has the veto.

_____

2. Since the U.N. was born, the number of its members has grown.

_____

Read the following selections and indicate whether the statements which follow are TRUE, FALSE, or NOT STATED in the passage:

Prussia must gather up her strength and maintain it in readiness for the opportune moment, which already has passed by several times. . . . Not by parliamentary speeches and majority votes are the great questions of the day determined—that was the great mistake of 1848 and 1849—but by iron and blood.

_____1. The speaker was prepared to use democratic means to further Germany's ambitions.
_____2. The speaker was Otto von Bismarck.
_____3. The speaker believed Germany had lost several opportunities.

_____
[4]*Ibid.*, pp. 43, 62.

These are some of the many variations to which the true-false question readily lends itself. Other variations will undoubtedly occur to other teachers. Notice that the variations lend themselves especially to the development of skill activities in which the student is required to show his understanding of a reading selection, map, cartoon, and statistical data, as well as a host of charts, graphs, and pictures.

The Matching Question

The format of the familiar and widely used matching question consists of two or perhaps three columns in which the student is asked to match the data in one column with corresponding or related data in another column. Properly prepared, this type of question can be genuinely effective in testing whether or not the student sees relevant relationships among classifications of data or can associate people and events, books and ideas, or any other association the teacher deems desirable to test. The following are the more important rules for effective preparation of matching questions:

- **Be sure the items in either column represent a homogeneous classification.** A common denominator should exist among the items, and it should be possible for the teacher to put a subhead above at least one of the columns.

Column A	Column B
___ 1. Diderot	A. Opposed mercantilism, favored *laissez-faire* in economics.
___ 2. Locke	B. Although born free, man was in chains.
___ 3. Montesquieu	C. Urged separation of powers among three government branches.
___ 4. Rousseau	D. Ridiculed the French and urged religious tolerance.
___ 5. Adam Smith	E. Wrote the first novel in the English language.
___ 6. Voltaire	F. Government based on the will of the people as expressed in majority rule.
	G. Led the Encyclopedists.

• **In order to expedite taking the test, the lists of items should be so arranged that the student can select the answer he or she wants quickly.** The lists should be relatively short; or, if it is necessary to have a relatively long list, it should have some kind of discernible, logical, or alphabetical order so that the student can quickly identify those items he or she wishes to select.

• **To reduce the possibilities of guessing, one list should be longer than the other and any possible clues should be eliminated.**

A modification of the matching question is one in which the student is asked to match three columns instead of two. An example of such a question follows:

Next to each name in Column A write the NUMBER of the country in Column B and the LETTER of the idea in Column C with which he was associated.

Column A	Column B	Column C
___ ___ Bismarck	1. Austria	A. Led the conservative movement of the mid-nineteenth century.
___ ___ Kemal	2. Prussia	B. Urged the modernization of his country and the reform of its government.
___ ___ Metternich	3. Russia	C. Successfully led the revolt of his people from Austrian domination.
___ ___ Mazzini	4. Spain	D. Generally regarded as the spirit of the unification movement.
___ ___ Cavour	5. Italy	E. Led his country to unity through a policy of blood and iron.
	6. Turkey	F. Joined the Crimean War in order to further the unification of his country.
	7. Belgium	

The Multiple-Choice Question

Although not without its faults, the multiple-choice question is probably the most effective short-answer type of question available to the world history teacher. It requires the student to select the number or letter of the answer that best completes the statement or best answers the question from among four or five possible choices. Because of its format, the multiple-choice question de-emphasizes rote recall and requires that the student be able to select the correct answers from those choices given him. Properly constructed, this kind of question lends itself to the measurement of growth in world history skills, the ability to relate cause and result, and the ability to discriminate from among a number of reasonable possibilities. So sophisticated has the art of writing multiple-choice questions become that those addicted to them deny the necessity of writing essay questions, thus avoiding the subjectivity in grading which enters the picture whenever the essay question is used.

Many of the rules covering the writing of other short-answer questions apply to multiple-choice questions. In particular, the multiple-choice question requires simple and unambiguous language, as well as the avoidance of specific determiners, such as "never," "always," "all," or "none." The following are some of the significant rules to help teachers write good multiple-choice questions:

• **For the stem of the statement, ask a question or use an incomplete sentence, whichever is more logical.**
• **Provide at least four options from which the student is to choose.**
• **Make these options seem reasonable alternatives as possible correct answers.**
• **Make the options provided approximately equal in length.**
• **Be sure that each item has only one correct answer.** Thus, "Which does not belong in the group: (a) Fourier, (b) Blanc, (c) Louis Philippe, (d) Owen?" If the classification the teacher had in mind was Utopian

Socialists, then Louis Philippe would be the answer. But if the students believed that the common denominator among the group was the fact that three were Frenchmen and one was an Englishman, they could make a good case for arguing that their answer, Owen, was perfectly correct.

• **Make the options grammatically appropriate so that the stem and the option complete a single thought.**

Thus we have the types of questions teachers may use to test and evaluate students. The essay question enables teachers to determine the creativity of the students' thinking processes, as well as their organizational ability. The short-answer question enables the teacher to measure the students' grasp of factual material, although properly prepared short-answer questions can measure more than merely memorized information. The essay question should be relatively broad; but it should, at the same time, suggest the organization and the depth required in the answer for a perfect score. Short-answer questions enable the teacher to cover broad fields of knowledge; and, because they tap a variety of aspects of the subject to be tested, they provide a superior sampling of the material in which the student is to be examined. Because they do so, they contribute materially to the reliability of the test, provided, of course, that the questions have been effectively prepared initially.

Using Test Results

Early in this chapter we pointed out that a test was a tool of teaching (a silent teacher) and a device of evaluation (an instrument of academic bookkeeping). The results of tests should be used to further both of these testing purposes. As a silent teacher, the test can serve to instruct both teacher and pupil. It can tell the teacher how well he or she has taught; which items the majority of the class seemed to understand; and which areas of study required further effort or remedial work. An item analysis of each question can be made to determine the order of difficulty, or to see how many students gave incorrect answers to each item. This might form the basis of review lessons.

An item analysis not only shows the teacher the number of students who got each question right or wrong, but it also enables him or her to build up a file of questions that effectively ranks the members of the class. That is, if 25 per cent of the highest papers are grouped and the items analyzed, and a similar quantity of the lowest papers are grouped and the items analyzed, an item analysis of a question that effectively measures relative ability and rank in class would reveal that a majority of the able students got the answer right, while a majority of the poor students got the answer wrong. Such a question is commonly regarded as effective in any examination in which an effort is made to rank students in order of ability.

Because item analyses are time-consuming, they are not often undertaken; but a considerable amount of time can be saved if an item analysis is undertaken with the class. By simply asking, "How many got question one wrong? Raise your hands," teachers can count the number wrong and subtract this from the number taking the test to get the number right. Teachers can then record the results on a master copy of the examination. This kind of analysis can be used for remedial work on those questions that troubled a large number of students, and a file can be built up of questions that seemed effectively to measure relative ability and rank in class. By placing questions so analyzed on index cards together with the results, each teacher will eventually build up his or her own file of effective test items.

Statistical analyses of many kinds may be made with the results of any examination. But admittedly this is not required for most teachers, since they usually give tests with sufficient frequency and get to know their students with sufficient intimacy to be able to judge each one and to have a keen insight into the relative standing of the students as a whole. Nevertheless, some very elementary statistical computations might be appropriate; these, posted and graphed in the classroom, give the class a progress report and provide incentive to do better.[5]

[5]See: Educational Testing Service, *Short-Cut Statistics for Teacher-Made Tests*. Princeton, New Jersey: Educational Testing Service, 1960; and Edward Arthur Townsend and Paul J. Burke, *Statistics for the Classroom Teacher*. New York: The Macmillan Company, 1963.

9

A World History Outline for a Year's Course

As the door burst open, Mr. Saxon, the teacher of World History II, rushed breathlessly into his room, having arrived five minutes late from lunch. He made frantic and relatively effective efforts to quiet a rather disorderly class which had begun to hope that Mr. Saxon would not be in at all today.

The teacher turned to the board to write the assignment for the next day, and the class proceeded to copy it into their notebooks, albeit with a certain amount of grumbling and disappointment. Fifteen minutes of the period had now elapsed, and by this time Mr. Saxon was ready to get a lesson under way. He had had in mind for some time a lesson on the "opening" of Africa by Stanley and Livingstone.

Mr. Saxon: Albert Schweitzer has been called a modern Livingstone. To what extent is this comparison justified? (*He calls on Susan Jones*.)

Susan: Who's Schweitzer?

Mr. Saxon: Does anyone know who Schweitzer was?

John: Wasn't he a missionary or something?

Mr. Saxon: What do you mean "or something"? Can you help us, Jim?

Jim: Well, Schweitzer did some medical work at Lambaréné.

Mary: *(Calling out)*: Who's Lambaréné?

Mr. Saxon *(Frowning)*: Don't call out, Mary, but the question really should have been "Where's Lambaréné?" Can anyone locate Lambaréné for us? Would you try it, Sam?

(Sam saunters slowly to the world map in front of the room; he looks all over it but with particular attention on South America.)

Mr. Saxon: Can someone help Sam? (*Alfred waves his hand wildly and is recognized*.)

(Alfred swaggers to the world map and locates Lambaréné correctly.)

Mary *(Calling out from the fourth seat of the fifth row)*: I can't see it from here.

Mr. Saxon: Show Mary Lambaréné again, Alfred.

Alfred *(Pointing)*: It's right here in Africa.

Mary: It's so small we can hardly see it on the map.

Mr. Saxon: You are right, Mary. I should have brought in a map of Africa, but we'll have it tomorrow. Well, what was Schweitzer doing in Africa? Alex?

Alex *(Authoritatively)*: Schweitzer was a genius who was a master organist and scholar but who decided, at the age of thirty, to give up his career to help the people of Africa. After studying medicine for seven years, he went to Lambaréné and I think he died there.

Mr. Saxon: Excellent, Alex. That was a fine statement. Yes, Schweitzer worked until he was over ninety years old. (*He recognizes Patricia, who has been waving her hand rather persistently*.) Yes, Patricia?

Patricia: Why would anyone give up a promising career as a scholar and a composer to suffer in Africa? I know I wouldn't.

Mr. Saxon: Well, how do the rest of you feel?

And so the discussion continues until the bell, when Mr. Saxon remarks, "When you come in tomorrow, class, let's consider why Albert Schweitzer has been called a modern Livingstone."

As a possible guideline in the teaching of world history, a number of suggestions are made below as to what to emphasize in each of three major units, what activities for the student might be provided, and what questions the teacher of world history might ask. It should be remembered that these are suggestions only, and they are offered only in the hope that perhaps one or two clues taken from these pages may on occasion help the teacher over the rough spots which are so frequently encountered in the planning and the teaching of world history.

The Ancient World

Points of Emphasis

1. Students should be encouraged to realize that there were many cradles of civilization: in the Middle East to be sure, but also in the Far East of China and in the Far West of what became Latin America. The geographic factors that best explain the growth and development of these ancient civilizations require examination in terms of geographic advantages and limitations.

2. The response of ancient civilizations to their environments contributed to cultural and technological innovation in the form of the development usually of a calendar, methods of transportation and navigation, and processes of mathematics, astronomy, and metallurgy.

3. The influence of religion on early people should be evaluated with particular emphasis on the role of the Judeo-Christian traditions of the West and the origins and influence of Moslem, Buddhist, and Hindu religions.

4. The nature of ancient political systems should be examined, and recognition should be made of the fact that in most ancient societies democracy as we understand that term did not exist, even in the "democracy" of ancient Athens.

5. The indebtedness of the modern world to the ancient one requires study, as does an appreciation of the cultural contributions of the ancient civilizations to art and architecture, literature, and music.

6. That humankind's sojourn on earth is relatively brief and that the era of history is but a moment of time should be amply demonstrated.

Suggested Activities

● To show that history is but a moment when measured against the longer period of time people lived on earth, draw a horizontal line on the chalkboard and ask students to come to the board and mark off on that line the portion of it that, in their judgment, represents the era of recorded history. For most students, it will come as a surprise to see that (depending upon the length of the line originally drawn) the portion of the line that may be regarded as the historical era is almost invisible to students sitting in the rear of the room.

● After studying those factors that help explain the development of Egyptian civilization, have the students try to discover for themselves other areas where, because of similar conditions, other cradles of civilization may be expected to develop; and ask the students to find the location of those areas that have such features and to identify the civilization which originated there.

● Using a cartoon showing Athenian society built upon a foundation of slavery, have students discuss how such a society can properly be regarded as democratic. Have students find the origin of some of our political and legal institutions in the Athenian system.

● Using the following selection from Plato's *Apology*, have students discuss its meaning and significance in terms of free speech in both ancient and modern times:

> And now Athenians, I am not going to argue for my own sake, as you may think, but for yours, that you may not sin against the God by condemning me, who am his gift to you. For if you kill me, you will not easily find a successor

RELATIONS BETWEEN OLD WORLD CIVILIZATIONS

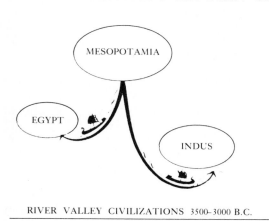

RIVER VALLEY CIVILIZATIONS 3500–3000 B.C.

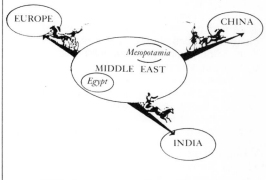

ANCIENT CIVILIZATIONS 1700–1400 B.C.

to me, who, if I may use such a ludicrous figure of speech, am sort of a gadfly given to the state by God; and the state is a great and noble steed who is tardy in his motions owing to his very size, and requires to be stirred into life. I am that gadfly which God has attached to the state; and all day long and in all places am always fastening upon you, arousing and persuading and reproaching you. You will not easily find another like me and therefore I would advise you to spare me.[1]

• An effective way to start a unit on Rome is to use the map showing the growth of the Roman Empire and to have the students detect reasons that help explain Rome's growth. After exhausting the geographic factors, see what other factors may be properly used in explanation.

• A student report on Jesus as an historical personage and the ideas of the early Christian church would be appropriate if followed by a discussion of why these doctrines appealed to many people of the Roman Empire at that time.

• In order to approach the study of India as still another cradle of civilization, exten-

sive use should be made of the map. Relations between Mesopotamia, Egypt, India, Europe, and China during ancient times (3000–1400 B.C.) may be illustrated by using the diagram found in McNeill's *Rise of the West*[2] (see above).

• Special reports on the contributions of India to civilization in music, science, and mathematics (so-called Arabic numbers, for example) should prove to be both interesting and illustrative of the fact that our modern civilization owes a debt to the East as well as to the West.

• In addition to a map study similar to that suggested for India above, the study of China might be approached through a reading of *The Travels of Marco Polo*. There are many good editions. The following description by Marco Polo of the China he knew may be read to the class, and its significance in terms of China's greatness can be discussed:

Upon the return of the grand khan to his capital, he holds a great and splendid court, which lasts three days, in the course of which he

[1]Saxe Commins and Robert N. Linscott, eds., *The Social Philosophers*. New York: Random House, 1947, pp. 199–200.

[2]William H. McNeill, *The Rise of the West*. Chicago: © 1963 by the University of Chicago Press, p. 169. Used with permission.

gives feasts and otherwise entertains those by whom he is surrounded. . . . The multitude of inhabitants and number of houses in the city, as also in the suburbs without the city . . . is greater than the mind can comprehend.

To this city everything that is most rare and valuable in all parts of the world finds its way; and more especially does this apply to India, which furnishes precious stones, pearls, and various drugs and spices. From the provinces of Cathay itself as well as from the other provinces in the empire, whatever there is of value is carried thither, to supply the demands of those multitudes who are induced to establish their residence in the vicinity of the court. The quantity of merchandise sold there exceeds also the traffic of any other place, for no fewer than a thousand carriages and pack-horses loaded with raw silk, make their daily entry; and gold tissues and silks of various kinds are manufactured to an immense extent.[3]

While this is not, of course, a description of China during ancient times, it can nevertheless be used as a point of departure to describe those factors that help to explain why China was able to develop an advanced civilization which, during the thirteenth century, was substantially more sophisticated than that of Europe.

• The significance of China's Great Wall may be compared with that of the pyramids of ancient Egypt.

Discussion Questions

In the section above, approaches to various significant aspects of the study of the ancient world were suggested. Of necessity, these were random illustrations that have been used successfully. In a similar vein, what follows are suggestions for possible discussion questions. These questions are designed to show that the world history lesson is not a matter of telling, but a matter of encouraging self-discovery and exploration by asking questions which impale the students on the horns of a dilemma and require of them thoughtful responses, as they try to solve the problem or search for the answer.

• **For a Lesson on the Nature of History.** "History is lies men have agreed upon." "History is bunk." These are some definitions that have been given to history. How do you account for the fact that some people have felt this way? Do you agree or disagree with these definitions? Why or why not? What does this tell us about the nature of history? How would you define history?

• **On Ancient Egypt.** The statement has been made that the average person would be just as comfortable in Egypt in 1900 B.C. as he would in Europe or America in 1900 A.D. Would you agree or disagree with this statement? Give evidence to support your point of view.

• **On Ancient Greece.** Socrates was ordered to drink poison because he was accused of "corrupting" the youth of Athens. What do you think he was telling them? What defects in Athenian society do you think Socrates criticized? Why has Socrates been described as a martyr to free speech?

• **On Ancient Rome.** The poet Byron said, "While stands the Colosseum Rome shall stand; when falls the Colosseum Rome shall fall." Is the Colosseum a well chosen symbol of Rome's greatness? Why or why not?

• **On India.** In the history of Greece and Rome which you have so far studied, you can see the beginnings or republicanism and democracy. Can the same be said for the history of India? Why or why not?

• **On China.** Our own age has been marked by a certain reluctance to change with new developments, such as space travel and nuclear power. Are we any more or less reluctant to change than the Chinese? Justify your viewpoint.

The Transition from Medieval to Modern Times

This unit of work ordinarily forms a significant part of the traditional course in world history. This is understandable in view of the fact that the Middle Ages and the Renaissance represent a watershed for the history of our own times. However, we urge that these centuries be treated quickly, largely for the purposes of providing historical continuity within the course, so that appropriate emphasis may be given to the backgrounds of recent events in Eastern, African, Latin American, as well as Western history. Included below are many more

[3]Manuel Komroff, ed., *The Contemporaries of Marco Polo*. New York: Liveright, 1953, pp. 152–153.

points of emphasis than can possibly be accomplished within the limitations suggested above; nevertheless, they are made here so that teachers may choose from among them according to their own judgment of what their students require and in terms of the requirements of their schools.

Points of Emphasis

1. Using broad brush strokes, indicate the nature of the medieval period as an age dominated by the Church and characterized politically by feudalism and economically by a primitive agricultural system.

2. Contrast the relative immaturity of medieval Europe to the sophisticated cultures of both East Asia, particularly in China, and the Byzantine and Moslem world.

3. A fine opportunity may be taken at this point to consider the historical development and basic ideas of Judaism, Christianity, and Islam.

4. Using broad brush strokes once again, treat the Renaissance as a transitional period in which cultural growth was accelerated (rather than "reborn"), in which the monopolistic position of the Church was broken, in which trade and commerce grew, and in which a new world was discovered.

Suggested Activities

If we keep in mind that these eras are to be treated concisely mainly to provide continuity, those techniques should be utilized that survey large portions of the unit and leave the student with a number of big ideas rather than isolated facts. This approach lends itself rather well to the team-teaching technique in which two or three teachers prepare a stimulating illustrated lecture on some significant aspects of the unit; each teacher then presents his or her lecture to the three classes at one time. Among the other procedures that we might suggest, the following have been found to be among the more successful:

• Have the students read, or perhaps read to them, selected portions of the *Arabian Nights* ("Aladdin and His Lamp," "Ali Baba and the Forty Thieves"); and discuss with them what these stories seem to reveal about the nature of Moslem society.

• Assign, either in class or for homework, the preparation and presentation of a travel folder which describes the sights in such Moslem cities as Cairo, Baghdad, Teheran. Illustrations may be clipped from old magazines or newspapers for the purpose of examining the architecture and comparing it with that of the Gothic church.

• Student reports on aspects of Moslem or Byzantine civilizations are often effective here, as are reports on the subject "If I Were a Feudal Knight."

• A round-table discussion on the merits of life in a medieval town as compared with life on a medieval manor is an effective procedure when the participants are properly prepared.

• Certainly, if time permits, one or more sessions should be spent in map study in which you examine with the class medieval routes of trade or the routes of the Crusaders.

• For the art of the Renaissance, a well decorated room with reproductions of the works of some of the masters would do much to set the tone for your lessons. Student reports on the work of Leonardo da Vinci, Michelangelo, and Raphael would likewise be appropriate.

• Leonardo da Vinci as a "man of the Renaissance," a man who could do many things well, is an excellent title for an extended biographical treatment in which Leonardo da Vinci as an inventor, military genius, stage designer, as well as artist, may be developed. The International Business Machines Corporation has a display of models of da Vinci's inventions, including his flying machine, which is available on a loan basis to schools.

• The possibilities of using the textbook or another source to read about the Reformation in order to understand its place in history and at the same time to develop skills of note-taking or of outlining should not be overlooked.

Discussion Questions

• **For a Lesson on Byzantium.** Why did Byzantium regard itself as the "heir of Rome"?

• **On Islam.** Samarkand was a trade center and a meeting place between Western and Chinese cultures. If you were in a bazaar in Samarkand, what would you buy? Why would you buy it?

• **On the Medieval Church.** (a) The medieval period has been described as the Age of Faith. Why? (b) How does the role of religion today differ from its role in medieval Europe?

• **On Feudalism.** (a) In the game of chess, you know that the king, queen, bishops, and knights are among the more powerful pieces. To what extent does this accurately reflect the feudal pyramid? (b) Was the chivalric code of honor honorable? Why or why not?

• **On Medieval Guilds.** If you were a shopper in medieval days, would the craft or merchant guilds help or hurt you in your efforts to get the most for your money? Why?

• **On the Renaissance.** (a) The ability to do many things well was a characteristic of Renaissance man. Is this a characteristic of great people of our own day? Justify your position. (b) The Renaissance has been described as a "bridge" to modern times. Would a man of the Renaissance be more at home had he lived during the Middle Ages or in our own age? Justify your view.

• **On the Reformation.** Luther posted his theses on the door of the Wittenberg Cathedral to make them known. How would a modern Luther make his views known?

The World Today

In any world history course, probably the greatest emphasis must be placed on the developments of modern times, roughly the nearly five hundred or so years since the discovery of America. We know these events in greater detail because they are more recent and closer to the times in which we live, and surely the student too should be familiar with the significant movements that have taken place: the rise of industrialism; the growth of democracy, as we know it, and the persistent challenges to democracy; the great movements of nationalism and imperialism; the great wars that have been waged and the earnest efforts that have been made to banish war; and the peaceful progress of humankind in science and technology, literature, music, and art.

Of particular interest at this time is the expansion of Europe, which brought Europeans into close contact with Africa, Asia, and Latin America; the abrasive nature of that contact requires ample treatment. Some areas of Africa, such as the Congo (Zaire) and some areas of Asia, such as China and Japan and Vietnam, should be examined as case studies of contrasting interests, ambitions, and traditions. While some time should indeed be taken to review significant current affairs, not so much time should be taken that an examination of the background of current problems is sacrificed.

Points of Emphasis

1. The point that the Age of Discovery of the fifteenth century was as significant and as exciting as the lunar probes are in our own time should be illustrated and developed.

2. The revolutionary nature of the modern world deserves substantial study and should include a brief treatment of the Glorious Revolution and the American Revolution and more detailed treatments of the French Revolution and the Russian Revolution. In the main, the important question to raise here is: Why do people revolt? Are the conditions which brought about the French Revolution and the Russian Revolution still factors in Asia and Africa? Revolution as a means of ameliorating longstanding grievances also requires evaluation.

3. The significance of mass production made possible by the Agricultural Revolution and the Industrial Revolution deserves extended development. Included in this treatment should be a survey of the classical economists, as well as a review of utopian and scientific socialist teachings. The pivotal role of Marx and the influence of socialism require study.

4. The examination of intellectual developments should go beyond a consideration of the work of the *philosophes*, and should include significant contributions in science, literature, music, and art of later centuries and of areas other than European.

5. The motives for imperialist expansion should be considered, and the "old" imperialism (sixteenth century) should be compared with the "new" imperialism (nineteenth century).

6. The unification of Germany should be

reviewed as a case study of nationalism as a unifying force, while that of Austria-Hungary might be studied as an example of nationalism as a divisive force. A study of the unification movement provides some background to help understand the German position in World War I, the rise of Hitler, and World War II.

7. If China is used as a case study of an East Asian society, then its geographic features should be reviewed, Europe's interest in China surveyed, and the forces within China working for expulsion of Europeans and modernization of China examined. China's failure to establish a genuinely united country under either Sun Yat-sen or Chiang Kai-shek should be explained in order to help students understand why the climate ripened for the conquest by the communists.

8. If India is studied, there are two parallel treatments that should be considered. First: India is a good example of imperialism at its best in many ways, in that Britain brought many technological improvements and advantages and granted a measure of self-government which gradually grew. Second: India is also a fine illustration of the refusal of a conquered people to be satisfied with concessions, so that only a total separation would be acceptable to them. The tactics of Gandhi and their adaptation by others seeking improvement in their lot deserve elaboration. The heritage of Gandhi in bringing about the fall of Indira Gandhi should be examined.

9. The causes of war, particularly as they apply to World Wars I and II, require some treatment; but more important are the fundamental sources of conflict among nations.

10. The factors that explain the growth of Fascism, Nazism, and Communism require analysis, with particular emphasis on the last two.

11. The interdependence of the modern world, the growth of regional associations such as NATO and the Common Market, and the role of the League of Nations and of the United Nations need to be examined.

It is obvious that all of the above cannot be studied in detail. But it must be the responsibility of the teacher to make a professional judgment of what to include and what to delete. Moreover, other areas not suggested here (e.g., Southeast Asia) deserve extended treatment. The course of study in world history should provide an opportunity to combat the Europocentric fallacy upon which most world history courses are based and to provide a background for the study of contemporary world affairs.

Suggested Activities

Because the subject area here is so broad, the suggested activities are offered in hopes that they may be found to be useful examples which may be adapted to a variety of classes and in a number of content areas.

• Certainly, a map study is an appropriate and effective way to examine the Age of Discovery and Exploration of the fifteenth and sixteenth centuries. The routes can be traced on outline maps, and the purpose of each voyage can be considered. Moreover, the climate of the Age of Discovery can be compared with the climate in our own day, when the goal appears to be nothing less than celestial navigation.

• Some students might enjoy preparing reports on the great battles of the Hundred Years' War. The introduction of gunpowder during that war and the beginning of the training of a yeoman army, as opposed to an army of knights, can be considered.

• Have the class prepare a newspaper for any given date, say between 1550 and 1650, in which significant political or economic developments are headlines; but in which some space is also taken to describe the lives of ordinary men and women. Some illustrations might even be drawn to show the dress of the day, the sports that were enjoyed, and the food that was eaten.

• The reign of Louis XIV is an excellent case study of the advantages and liabilities of absolutism. This might be developed through some of the writings of Saint-Simon, thus introducing students to the use of memoirs in reconstructing the past.

• If the *philosophes* of the Age of Reason are to be studied at all, a fine procedure is to use some of the readings found in Louis L. Snyder's *The Age of Reason*[4] as a means

---

[4]Louis L. Snyder, *The Age of Reason*. New York: D. Van Nostrand Company, Inc., 1955.

of examining the revolutionary implications of their remarks.

• Examination of the actual *cahiers* that were written likewise forms a good point of departure for an examination of the alleged causes of the French Revolution.

• To evaluate the role of Napoleon, hold a mock trial. Have the class draw up a charge that might be made against Napoleon and have two students serve as defense and prosecution attorneys. Witnesses might be summoned by either of the attorneys, as attempts are made to evaluate Napoleon's domestic reforms and foreign adventures.

• The Congress of Vienna lends itself to a dramatization in which each member of the class can play a role. The leading figures should, of course, be represented; and a measure of spontaneity should be encouraged, so that students can understand the problems of getting consensus in a large meeting and the opportunity that this provides for the few to assume the role of leadership.

• Developing related library skills is among the responsibilities of the world history teacher. To combine these with an appreciation of the significance of great books by authors such as Anatole France, Galsworthy, Zola, Charles Darwin, Dickens, Dumas, Tagore, Buck, Sachs, Baldwin, and others, have the students go to the library, where either the teacher or the librarian can give a lesson in the use of the card catalog. Often the use of the vertical file can likewise be encouraged in this way.

• Map studies are highly important in studying problems of imperialistic expansion. Students should learn how to read map symbols and should get some idea of the extent of the empires and the great nations of Europe.

• The opportunity to invite guest speakers to class should not be overlooked. This is an especially effective way to change the pace of instruction, especially when introducing case studies of China, Japan, India, or a Latin American country. In this area, students who may come from these countries are often extremely effective in explaining the point of view of their country of origin.

• Newspaper facsimiles of front pages of the past (often provided by *The New York Times*) are useful for the purposes of discussing the crises that made headlines prior to both World Wars.

• The biographical approach is also effective for such individuals as Clemenceau, Orlando, Lloyd George, Wilson, Pershing, Kaiser Wilhelm, Hindenburg, Hitler, Mussolini, and Stalin.

• To provide variety and to develop reading and study skills, do not overlook the possibilities of supervised study lessons in which students might read about the rise of dictatorship and be asked to outline it or to take notes on it. This is a device useful for slower students and can provide the needed scholarly background for effective follow-up discussion.

• In examining the rise of dictatorship, quotes are useful in sparking class discussion—for example, Hitler's "Today we own Germany, tomorrow the world!" and "The German race has higher rights than all others"; or Mussolini's "When I hear the word liberty, I reach for my gun!"

• In discussing and studying more recent history, newspaper headlines often furnish useful points of departure, since many of the problems of twenty or even fifty or more years ago are still unresolved. Thus, for a study of Soviet dictatorship, some of Khrushchev's quips ("We'll bury you!") or problems of communism today may be used as points of departure for a study of the origins of the current struggle. Current Sino-Soviet conflict has its origins in events that go far back to Russian-Chinese relationships under Sun Yat-sen and probably earlier, and these events can be used in discussing Soviet or Chinese communism and Soviet-Chinese conflict.

• Current newspaper headlines are good points of departure for study and investigation of the problems of *détente*, disarmament, and the United Nations.

Discussion Questions

• **For a Lesson on Napoleon.** (a) H. G. Wells said of Napoleon: "The figure he makes in history is one of incredible self-conceit, vanity, greed, cunning, of callous contempt of all who trusted him; and of a grandiose aping of Caesar, which would be purely comic if it were not caked over with human blood." Is this a fair evaluation of

Napoleon? Defend your point of view. (b) Napoleon is said to have set France "right side up" but turned Europe "upside down." To what extent is this true or false? (c) Why might Napoleon's wars with England be called a battle between a "tiger and a shark?"

• **On the Revolutions of 1820, 1830, and 1848.** (a) What is meant by the saying "When France has a cold, all Europe sneezes?" (b) H. G. Wells· said, "The right to vote by itself is a useless thing." How does the election of Louis Napoleon in France prove the truth of the statement? (c) Patriotism has been called the "last refuge of the scoundrel." Is this fair? Why or why not? (d) The Glorious Revolution of 1688, the American Revolution of 1776, the French Revolution of 1789, and the Russian Revolution of 1917 are among the historic turning points in world affairs. Should the Latin American revolutions be regarded in the same light? Why or why not?

• **On the Emergence of Japan.** (a) Mutsuhito reigned in Japan while Victoria reigned in England. Why might Mutsuhito have found much to admire in nineteenth-century England? (b) Japan has been called the "Prussia of East Asia." Why? (c) Japan has been called the "Britain of the Pacific." Why?

• **On China.** (a) Sun Yat-sen has been called the "George Washington of China." To what extent are the roles of the two heroes the same or different? (b) "The Chinese communists behave the way they do because they are Chinese, not because they are communists." To what extent would you agree or disagree with this statement? (c) Chinese law was often unfair in Western eyes. Was this sufficient reason for demanding the rights of extraterritoriality? Give reasons for your point of view.

• **On Africa.** (a) John Gunther's *Inside Africa* says, "Africa is aflame with nationalism." What did he mean? What evidence in current affairs proves that the statement is as true today as when it was written? (b) Africa lies close to Europe (illustrate on map), yet until recent centuries it remained a little known continent. How do you account for this? (c) One often hears the remark that African nations are "not ready for self-government." What does readiness mean in

this case? Who decides when a nation is ready for self-government?

• **On India.** (a) Was the "invasion" of India by Europe any better or worse than the invasion of India by Indo-Aryans, Huns, or Moslems? Explain your point of view. (b) To what extent is the old caste system of India the same or different from segregation as it exists in the United States? Does it resemble or differ from *apartheid* as practiced in South Africa? (c) One hundred years after the Sepoy Mutiny, India was free. India felt independence had come slowly. Britain felt it had come quickly. With which side do you agree most? Why?

• **On World War I.** On board: "Europe for half a century had indulged in an orgy of *nationalism, imperialism, militarism* that could have no end but war; and in this no nation was guiltless." To what extent would you agree or disagree? Are the italicized terms fundamental or immediate causes of World War I? Why? Give illustrations to prove each of the italicized terms.

• **On Results of World War I.** (a) The statement has been made, "To the victor belong the spoils." Meaning? Is this a sound principle on which to end a war? Why or why not? (b) To what extent are the Fourteen Points reflected in the Treaty of Versailles? (c) The period between World War I and World War II has been called the Long Armistice. Why?

• **On Fascism.** The historian Louis Snyder wrote in *The World of the Twentieth Century*:

> Mussolini introduced a series of reforms. He drastically revised the system of taxation and finance, refunded foreign debts, stabilized the currency. He enacted high tariffs, expanded the merchant marine and concluded trade pacts with foreign countries. His extensive program of public works was designed to increase employment. He encouraged foreign capitalists to invest their funds in Italy, and he began a campaign to attract tourists. He reorganized the educational system in an effort to combat illiteracy. . . . The power-hungry dictator attempted to give his people everything except the one thing without which human life becomes meaningless—freedom.[5]

[5]Louis L. Snyder, *The World in the Twentieth Century*. Princeton, New Jersey: D. Van Nostrand Company, 1955, p. 80.

In view of these efforts, does Mussolini deserve praise or blame? Was he the man Italy needed in its hour of trouble? Justify your point of view.

• (a) Koppel S. Pinson, an historian, wrote a book about Germany between 1933 and 1945, in which he had a chapter entitled "Germany Goes Berserk." Do you think this is a good title for the period in which Hitler came to power? Why or why not? (b) As reported by William L. Shirer in *The Rise and Fall of the Third Reich*, during Hitler's attempt to exterminate the Jews, Jews were made into soap in a recipe that called for "12 pounds of human fat, 10 quarts of water, and 8 ounces to a pound of caustic soda . . . all boiled for two or three hours and then cooled."[6] Is there any explanation for this callous treatment of human life? How do you account for the failure of many people in the rest of the world to intervene?

Characteristics and Examples of Daily Lesson Plans

The world history outline presented above must be further divided into units of work and into daily lesson plans. The lesson plan is an important tool of world history teaching. Its main characteristics may be identified as follows: the topic, the aim, sometimes a review, the motivation, the content outline, the pivotal questions, the summaries, and the application. Each of the elements of a daily lesson will be considered briefly in turn.

Topic: This represents a simple statement of the subject that the teacher is planning to consider for the day.

Aim: Each world history lesson should be three-dimensional in nature in that it must make a contribution to growth in students' knowledge and understanding; in work and study skills, as well as in the skills used by the historian; and in the ability to make appropriate value judgments.

Review: This segment of the lesson plan contains those provisions which have been made to fix knowledge and skills previously studied.

Motivation: This is designed to provide a springboard for the lesson and a point of departure for further study. The motivation serves to identify the aim of the lesson.

Content Outline: In the space provided for the content outline, a teacher who plans carefully writes the factual content of the material the class will study. In form, it might serve as a guide for the outline to be written on the chalkboard. The space might also include dates, names, and places that the class should know and that the teacher may not remember under the stress of the classroom.

Pivotal Questions: Medial summaries, which occur at appropriate points in the lesson, and the final summary, which occurs near its end, are designed to fix information and to draw together the various facets of the lesson.

Application: This portion of the lesson attempts to show the students how the material studied in the lesson may be applied to a problem in the contemporary world or may provide a better understanding of the past.

Advance Assignment: The assignment is the homework that world history students are expected to do in order to come to class somewhat familiar with the work to be discussed. While in some subjects the homework assignment is traditionally drill and reinforcement of what has been taught that day, in world history the assignment generally, but not always, takes the form of new work in preparation for the coming lesson. Because the success of a lesson in world history is so dependent upon how well the assignment has been studied, it is suggested that ample time be devoted to anticipating difficulties students might encounter. A discussion of the assignment should be held early in the lesson.

The lesson plan is only a guide, and it is not to be followed slavishly nor imposed arbitrarily. If class discussion leads to other avenues of significant and pertinent study, departure from the lesson plan is not only reasonable but is expected of the better teacher. Sidney Hook has included among his criteria of good teaching "the ability to plan a lesson without mechanically imposing it on the class. . . . What the teacher must aim at is to make each class hour an integrated experience with an aesthetic, if possible, a dramatic, unity of its own."[7]

---

[6]New York: Simon and Schuster, 1960, p. 971.

[7]Sidney Hook, *Education for Modern Man*. New York: Alfred A. Knopf, 1963, pp. 224–225.

THE GLORIOUS REVOLUTION OF 1688

Aim: How did the Glorious Revolution contribute to the growth of democracy? (To be elicited from class.)

Motivation: We are proud of the fact that ours is a democratic nation. What must a nation have to be democratic? Our lesson for today is on the Glorious Revolution. In view of these characteristics of democracy, what appropriate question does this raise as we study this topic?

OUTLINE

1628: Petition of Right
1. Taxes not to be levied without Parliament's approval.
2. No arbitrary appeal.

1679: Habeas Corpus Act
No person may be held in prison without a fair and quick trial.

1689: Bill of Rights
1. Anglican King
2. No interference with elections.
3. Right of petition.
4. No excessive bail.
5. Annual meetings of Parliament.
6. No standing army.
7. No taxes without Parliament's consent.

PIVOTAL QUESTIONS

1. Although the Tudors were able to rule the British household, the Stuarts were not. Why not?
2. Charles I was beheaded for the crimes of his father, as well as his own crimes. If you were prosecuting attorney at the trial of Charles I, what arguments against him would you use?
3. *Medial Summary:* Which of these grievances would the people find most serious? Arrange these grievances in order of importance.
4. Between 1603–1689 the British tried to remedy these conditions. To what extent were they successful?
5. The elevation of William and Mary was called a revolution. How could replacing one king with another be called a revolution? Why "Glorious"?
6. *Summary:* Consider what makes a country democratic. To what extent can England be considered democratic in 1689?
7. *Application:* To what extent are our election days indebted to the "Glorious Revolution"? Is "He who controls the purse strings rules the household" true in our own government?

SUGGESTED TIME LINE
(on board)

1603–1625	1625–1649	1660–1685	1685–1688
James I	Charles I	Charles II	James II
	Petition of Right	Habeas Corpus Act	Bill of Rights

THE MARCH OF DEMOCRACY IN BRITAIN

Aim: Did England make "full payment" on Democracy? (Elicited.)

Motivation: It has sometimes been said that England achieved democracy on the installment plan. To what extent is this true? If this is true, what problem for today does this suggest?

OUTLINE

Complaints (elicited)
1. Rotten and pocket boroughs.
2. Limited franchise.
3. House of Lords hereditary.
4. No secret ballot.

Chartist Program (elicited)
1. Secret ballot.
2. Equal electoral districts.
3. Annual parliaments.
4. Payment for members of Parliament.
5. Male suffrage.

March of Democracy in Britain (on board)
1829 Catholics eligible for Parliament.
1832 Middle class gets vote.
1858 Jews eligible for Parliament.
1867 City working class gets vote.
1872 Secret ballot.
1884 Country working class gets vote.
1918 All men, women over 30 can vote.
1928 All women can vote.

PIVOTAL QUESTIONS

1. In 1800, England was a model democracy, yet if you were living in England at that time you would have reason to complain. Why?
2. In view of these complaints, to what extent was England overdue in its "payments"?
3. Why might the Reform Bill of 1832 be considered England's "down payment" on democracy?
4. The Reform Bill of 1832 is important for what it did and for the way it was passed. Why?
5. If you were a Chartist, what further payments would you insist be made?
6. Were the demands of the Chartists reasonable or unreasonable? Why?
7. On the board is a summary of England's payment to democracy. Would you be satisfied? Why or why not?
8. If you compare the list of complaints in 1832 with the list of achievements, was England keeping up its "payments"?

Application: Can England's "bill" be marked "paid in full"? Why or why not? Why does democracy require constant additonal "payments"? Give evidence of this in England, in America. Elsewhere.

THE UNITED NATIONS

Aim: Can the United Nations guarantee world peace?

Motivation: (Riddle) "It is not a government. It is not a 'superstate.' It is an international organization dedicated to the cause of peace." What is it? Justify your answer. What does the riddle tell us about the powers of the United Nations? What problem for our study does it pose?

Development:

Content Outline and Materials	Pivotal Questions and Procedure
Articles of Confederation and United Nations Charter	1. In his book *Dress Rehearsal*, Carl Van Doren suggests that the government of the United States under the Articles of Confederation was a dress rehearsal for the United Nations. To what extent is such a comparison justified?
1. Articles of Confederation and United Nations Charter have neither executive, taxing, nor judicial powers.	
2. Articles of Confederation intended to be a national government, but the United Nations Charter, on either national or world levels, did not.	
League of Nations	2. From a study of the United Nations Organization, to what extent does it represent an improvement over the League of Nations?
1. Provision for withdrawal.	
2. No provision for armed force.	
3. Unanimity required in Security Council.	
United Nations	
1. No provision for withdrawal.	
2. Provision for armed force.	
3. Only permanent members have veto.	
Suggestions for Improving the United Nations	3. It is widely recognized that the United Nations is not a perfect organization and can be improved. What suggestions for improvement have been offered?
1. Abolition of veto.	4. To what extent would the changes listed strengthen the United Nations?
2. Proportional voting.	5. If you had to draw up a "score card" showing "hits and runs and errors" of the United Nations, how would the United Nations score? Justify your answer.
3. Three-person Secretariat.	
4. Enlarge Security Council.	
Medial Summary	
(List here the successes and failures of the United Nations.)	
Summary and Application	6. It has been said that the failure of the League was a failure of men not machinery. To what extent might the same thing happen to the United Nations?
	7. To what extent can the United Nations guarantee world peace? What tests is the United Nations likely to face? To what extent is it likely to pass those tests?

ORGANIZATIONS USEFUL IN THE TEACHING OF WORLD HISTORY

World history teachers often seek supplementary information to enrich their classroom instruction. Used creatively, resources such as pamphlets, charts, maps, and "teaching kits" can aid instruction. A number of organizations provide such material, often at no cost or for a minimal fee. Some of these organizations are identified below along with many of the materials and services they provide. Obviously, many other helpful organizations exist. Those mentioned here represent merely a basic core. Since prices of the materials they offer are subject to change, they are not included. Information on current prices and additional materials can be obtained by writing to the director of each organization.

• A good source for obtaining information about specific countries is through their embassy or consulate in this country. Nearly every nation maintains an embassy or consulate in Washington, D.C. Foreign consulates are also located in most major cities. Useful historical, cultural, and political information can be acquired from these agencies upon written request to their public affairs officer. Names and addresses of all embassy officials in Washington, D.C. can be found in the *Diplomatic List* available through the U.S. Government Printing Office. Consulates in major cities are listed in the telephone directory.

• The African-American Institute (866 United Nations Plaza, New York City 10017) publishes a variety of materials relevant to teaching about Africa. One of the more useful resources from this organization is a *Secondary Starter Kit*. Applicable for grades 7–12, this resource presents ideas, sources, maps, wall charts, and bibliographic references germane to teaching about Africa. An 85-page booklet, *Are You Going To Teach About Africa?* also presents a variety of suggestions and sources helpful to those incorporating the study of Africa into the classroom. A third publication, *Africa Report*, is a bimonthly magazine containing information on cultural and political life in Africa. The African-American Institute also supports a School Service Division that provides useful information and answers specific requests for information on instructional materials about Africa.

• American Universities Field Staff (3 Lebanon Street, Hanover, New Hampshire 03755) has published five teaching-learning units that present "patterns of culture in various societies around the world." The program confronts students with a range of perspectives on human cultures. It encourages their understanding of and empathy for varying global life styles and a reduction of their parochial attitudes. Units focusing on human culture from various perspectives ask students to "understand—not memorize; evaluate—not accept."

One of the major strengths of the Field Staff program is its flexibility. The units contain a variety of instructional media from cassette recordings and simulations to moral dilemmas for value analysis. Readings are geared to a variety of interest and ability levels from grade 4 through grade 12. Finally, the Field Staff units can be used separately as mini-courses or to supplement existing course material or in combination to form a basic program.

• Two organizations that are dedicated to promoting and improving the study of Asia are The Asia Society, Inc. (112 East 64th Street, New York City 10021) and the Association for Asian Studies (Ohio State University, 29 West Woodruff Avenue, Columbus, Ohio 43210). The Asia Society, Inc. publishes an informative quarterly journal, *Asia*, and a monthly *Calendar* identifying pertinent radio and television programs, films, and lectures. It also works with those organizations and individuals developing instructional materials on Asia. The Association for Asian Studies publishes a useful newsletter, *Focus*, and a series of occasional papers relevant to teaching about Asia. It is also concerned with assisting teachers in generating Asian Studies programs at the secondary level.

• The Center for Global Perspectives (218 East 18th Street, New York City 10003) is dedicated to "increasing public awareness and knowledge about our global society and its problems of conflict and social change." Its magazine, *Intercom* (published from three to five times yearly), provides instructional mini-units and creative teaching suggestions focusing on various global problems and developments. The bulk of recent issues has been devoted to classroom activities, although readings, context-setting essays, and annotations of various instructional materials are often included. Recent issues have dealt with teaching about such topics as population, multi-national corporations, and the future. The Center has also prepared multimedia instructional kits, such as *Patterns of Human Conflict* (New York: Center for War/Peace Studies, 1974).

• The Foreign Policy Association (345 East 46th Street, New York City 10017) is a non-profit organization seeking to improve understanding on global issues. Its *Headline Series*, a readable series of pamphlets published five times a year, provides a compact analysis of current international topics and issues. Each pamphlet contains useful maps, charts, discussion questions, and bibliographic references. A second source used widely at the secondary level is *Great Decisions*. This annual publication presents a series of articles focusing on major foreign policy topics. Applicable maps, charts, discussion questions and bibliographies are included. Finally, this agency's *New Dimensions* series provides teachers with helpful suggestions on teaching about world affairs.

• The Institute for World Order (11 West 42nd Street, New York City 10036) is a non-profit organization seeking to promote an understanding of the process and problems of creating world order. The Institute consults with schools and sponsors various conferences and seminars. Its School Program publishes a quarterly newsletter, *Progress Report*, and a monthly leaflet, *Ways and Means of Teaching About World Order*, which provide information on the Institute's programs and activities. A *Reprint* series presenting articles salient to global education is also available.

• The Overseas Development Council (1717 Massachusetts Avenue, N.W., Washington, D.C. 20036) is a non-profit organization seeking to foster an understanding of the variety of problems facing the world's developing nations. It has produced *Global Poverty and Development: A Resource Book for Educators*, a two-part work presenting ways to integrate a development perspective into traditional high school social studies courses. Readings, case studies, a film guide, and a listing of organizations and materials are also included. ODC also publishes two pamphlet series, *The Development Paper* and *Communique Series*, which focus on current development activities and problems.

by David D. Victor

Index

Illustration credits

Cover: Crystal Productions, Aspen, Colorado; page iv: Paul Conklin; pages 8, 54: Joe DiDio, National Education Association; page 14: Library of Congress; page 22: Ronald Horbinsky; page 30: U.S. Signal Corps; page 44: OEO, Michael D. Sullivan; page 52: From a New York State Education Department publication. Used with permission; page 64: Drawings by Robert Diamond, Syracuse University; page 74: NASA, Courtesy EPA.

Index prepared by Mary W. Matthews
Book design and production by Joseph Perez.
Typesetting by Byrd PrePress.
Printing and Binding by William Byrd Press.